MW00523051

GOD'S CONSTANT PRESENCE

True Stories of Everyday Miracles

Signs
& Wonders

EDITORS OF GUIDEPOSTS

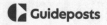

Signs & Wonders

Published by Guideposts
100 Reserve Road, Suite E200
Danbury, CT 06810
Guideposts.org

Copyright © 2023 by Guideposts. All rights reserved.

This book, or parts thereof, may not be reproduced, stored in a retrieval system, or transmitted in any form or by any means, electronic, mechanical, photocopying, recording or otherwise, without the written permission of the publisher.

Acknowledgments

Every attempt has been made to credit the sources of copyrighted material used in this book. If any such acknowledgment has been inadvertently omitted or miscredited, receipt of such information would be appreciated.

Scripture quotations marked (ESV) are taken from the *Holy Bible, English Standard Version*. Copyright © 2001 by Crossway Bibles, a division of Good News Publishers. Used by permission. All rights reserved.

Scripture quotations marked (ISV) are taken from the *Holy Bible, International Standard Version*. Copyright © 1995–2014 by ISV Foundation. All rights reserved internationally. Used by permission of Davidson Press, LLC.

Scripture quotations marked (KJV) are taken from the *King James Version of the Bible*.

Scripture quotations marked (MSG) are taken from *The Message*. Copyright © 1993, 1994, 1995, 1996, 2000, 2001, 2002 by Eugene H. Peterson.

Scripture quotations marked (NIV) are taken from *The Holy Bible, New International Version*. Copyright © 1973, 1978, 1984, 2011 by Biblica, Inc. Used by permission of Zondervan. All rights reserved worldwide. zondervan.com

Scripture quotations marked (NKJV) are taken from *The Holy Bible, New King James Version*. Copyright © 1982 by Thomas Nelson.

Scripture quotations marked (NLT) are taken from the *Holy Bible, New Living Translation*. Copyright © 1996, 2004, 2007 by Tyndale House Foundation. Used by permission of Tyndale House Publishers Inc., Carol Stream, Illinois. All rights reserved.

Scripture quotations marked (Tanakh) are taken from *Tanakh: A New Translation of the Holy Scriptures according to the Traditional Hebrew Text*. Copyright © 1985 by the Jewish Publication Society. All rights reserved.

Scripture quotations marked (TLB) are taken from *The Living Bible*. Copyright © 1971 by Tyndale House Publishers, Inc., Carol Stream, Illinois. All rights reserved.

Cover and interior design by Serena Fox Design Company

Cover photo by Shutterstock
Typeset by Aptara, Inc.

ISBN 978-1-961126-35-0 (hardcover)
ISBN 978-1-959633-05-1 (epub)

Printed and bound in the United States of America
10 9 8 7 6 5 4 3

Wonder encourages us to stand humbly before
the unfathomable mysteries of human life,
trusting that, in them, we encounter God.

–*Sister Melannie Svoboda, author*

TABLE *of* CONTENTS

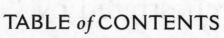

Orchestrated by God

By Kim Taylor Henry

WHEN OUR son was twenty-eight years old, he was diagnosed with cancer, told he had only six months to live, and to "get his affairs in order." The depth of the devastation we felt cannot be adequately described. I cried out to God. One morning I felt an impulse to step outside onto our back deck at a time when I normally would not have. There, directly in front of me, huge and commanding, were two contrails in the shape of a cross.

That was over twelve years ago. Our son is cancer free and has been for over ten years. I know that others have seen contrails form crosses, but I also know that time, it was for me, for us—orchestrated and sent by God. It was a Sign. God was with us. Everything would be all right. It was a Wonder.

Noah Webster's 1828 *American Dictionary of the English Language* (Foundation for American Christian Education; Facsimile of 1st edition: 1967) is scripturally influenced. It defines "sign" as "some visible transaction, event, or appearance intended as proof or evidence of something else," and "wonder" as "that emotion which is excited by…the presentation to the sight or mind, of something new, unusual, strange, great, extraordinary, or not well understood; something that arrests the attention by its novelty, grandeur, or inexplicableness," also, a "Cause of wonder."

Our God is not a distant deity with no direct involvement in our lives. He loves us deeply (Ephesians 3:14–18) and He cares about every detail of our days (Luke 12:7). As His Word assures us, He is with us always. Not occasionally, not even frequently, but *always* (Matthew 28:20). Not just with other people, but with you and me as well—with us, around us, in us. He declares, "Do not fear, for I am with you; do not be dismayed, for I am your God. I will strengthen you and help you; I will uphold you with my righteous right hand" (Isaiah 41:10, NIV). And He is and He does. Every day. In countless ways.

This book, *Signs & Wonders,* part of a series aptly titled "God's Constant Presence," provides beautiful confirmation of that truth. The stories shared in this book are vivid, moving, true-life examples recounted by everyday people like you and me who have experienced that soothing awareness that God is and has been with them always. Their accounts can help open our eyes, ears, and hearts to the reality that God will never leave us or forsake us either (Deuteronomy 31:6–8).

Often we don't think about that certainty or even realize it: "We may ignore, but we can nowhere evade, the presence of God. The world is crowded with Him. He walks everywhere incognito" (C. S. Lewis). But then there may occur a sign, a wonder, which might come as a jolt of awareness or as serene recognition. In whatever form it manifests, it speaks directly to our heart and assures us that "Yes, truly, He *is* with me, every minute, every day."

As the stories conveyed in this collection demonstrate, sometimes that realization occurs instantaneously, in the midst of our circumstances. We may feel a calm assurance, that "peace of God, which transcends all understanding" (Philippians 4:7, NIV). We may sense his presence: "Be still, and know that I am

God" (Psalm 46:10, NIV). We may feel a quieting of our soul: "The LORD your God is with you, the Mighty Warrior who saves. He will take great delight in you; in his love he will no longer rebuke you, but will rejoice over you with singing" (Zephaniah 3:17, NIV). Or He may lead us to something, someone, or someplace that exclaims to our spirit, "He is with me."

Other times the realization may register with us only in retrospect when we grasp that what occurred can only be explained through Him, could have happened no other way than from Him, and makes sense in no way except that it was Him with us, holding our hand, gently showing us the way, His way (Psalm 73:23). "The LORD is my shepherd, I lack nothing…he leads me beside quiet waters, he restores my soul. He guides me along the right paths for his name's sake" (Psalm 23:1–3, NIV).

Our experience, the sign or wonder we are sent, will be different in form or in timing than anything we could have planned or imagined: "'For my thoughts are not your thoughts, neither are your ways my ways,' declares the LORD. 'As the heavens are higher than the earth, so are my ways higher than your ways and my thoughts than your thoughts'" (Isaiah 55:8, 9, NIV).

The stories in *Signs & Wonders* show that God's way may be surprising or circuitous, but the destination is His will, and it is good: "This is what the LORD says—he who made a way through the sea…See, I am doing a new thing! Now it springs up; do you not perceive it? I am making a way in the wilderness and streams in the wasteland" (Isaiah 43:16, 19, NIV).

Signs and wonders will be inexplicable, except that we feel certain their origin was God, that they are or were God in action, and that He has been with us all along: "What no eye has seen, what no ear has heard, and what no human mind has conceived—the things God has prepared for those who love him" (1 Corinthians 2:9, NIV). It just may have taken that sign or wonder to open our eyes to His presence, causing us, like doubting Thomas, to exclaim, "My Lord and my God!" (John 20:28, ISV).

God may reveal Himself to us through other people, by putting them into our lives and our circumstances at just the right time to help us along the way:

> In their loving you, He was loving you. In their helping you, it was He who was helping you. And in their encouragement, it was He who was encouraging you… And as Mary Magdalene looked into the face of God but didn't realize it was His face, so too in your life you have looked into His face and not realized it was the face of God. But if you look, you'll see it. (Jonathan Cahn, *The Book of Mysteries*, Frontline, 2016, Day 298)

A sign and wonder may open our eyes to the fact that He is not only with us, but also lives *in* us. Jesus said, "I am in my Father, and you are in me, and I am in you" (John 14:20, NIV). This same message is found in John 14:16, 17; Ephesians 2:22; Colossians 1:27; 2 Timothy 1:14; and 1 Corinthians 3:16 and 6:19. His presence in us may be a gift to others as we act as His face, hands, feet, and body to them, making them aware of His presence. We may serve as His sign and wonder for them:

> Christ has no body now but yours. No hands, no feet on earth but yours. Yours are the eyes through which he looks compassion on this world. Yours are the feet with which he walks to do good. Yours are the hands through

which he blesses all the world. Yours are the hands, yours are the feet, yours are the eyes, you are his body. Christ has no body now on earth but yours. (Teresa of Avila)

The world is filled with signs and wonders from God. Everywhere, His creation points to Him and to His abiding presence. The sunshine and the rain, thunder and lightning, trees and flowers, fields and mountains, rivers, oceans, music—be it birdsong, voice, or symphony—laughter, a baby's silken skin and teeny fingers and toes, the complexity of our own bodies, and everyday miracles too vast to count. "I praise you because I am fearfully and wonderfully made; your works are wonderful, I know that full well" (Psalm 139:14, NIV).

Family, love, birth, marriage, the beauty of a crimson sunrise, the embrace of hazy dusk, the dazzle of the stars, the intricacy of snowflakes, the marvel of water, the unfathomable diversity of all He has designed, what we see, hear, smell, taste, and touch—all that our senses bring to us every day—are signs and wonders pointing to Him: "Am I not present everywhere, whether seen or unseen?" (Jeremiah 23:24, MSG). We need only observe and absorb, open our eyes and our hearts to what He has created, its infinite variety, complexity, and grandeur, to know that God is present in it all: "Since the creation of the world God's invisible qualities—his eternal power and divine nature—have been clearly seen, being understood from what has been made, so that people are without excuse" (Romans 1:20, NIV).

There are so many of God's signs and wonders surrounding us daily that we may become accustomed to them and fail to even notice or appreciate their message. We may take them in stride or for granted. We may become blind or deaf to them, or forget they speak loudly of the One who fashioned them.

There may come a time when God jolts us awake with a sign and a wonder of a magnitude we can't ignore. Sometimes that is what it takes to ignite our awareness of His presence: "I was blind but now I see" (John 9:25, NIV).

This ignition may occur in the joys of our life, when we realize a dream, accomplish a goal, laugh with delight, feel the love of family and the caring of friends, and revel in gifts of everyday life. During these occasions, we may be acutely aware that God is with us, also smiling, delighting in our enjoyment of that with which He has blessed us.

Our awakening may come in, or as a result of, one of life's storms, for "it is often in our darkest hour that the light of God's presence shines the brightest" (Unknown). We may experience an internal prompting, a stirring in our soul. Or we may receive exactly what we need when we need it, even if we didn't know we needed it! "Your Father knows what you need before you ask him" (Matthew 6:8, NIV).

Our sign and wonder may come at a time of great fear or uncertainty. It will say to us, "Do not be afraid; do not be discouraged, for the LORD your God will be with you wherever you go" (Joshua 1:9, NIV). It may be in the form of unexplained peace (John 14:27). It may come in answer to our fervent prayers (James 5:16). It may even come to those who have rejected Him. A Godsent sign and wonder may serve as the avenue through which their eyes and hearts open to Him, bringing an understanding that "All which I took from thee I did but take, Not for thy harms, But just that thou might'st seek it in My arms" ("The Hound of Heaven," Francis Thompson, 1890).

A sign and a wonder may come to us when we have neglected to turn to God and are struggling on our own: "He reached down from on high and took hold of me; he drew me out of deep waters" (Psalm 18:16, NIV). It may be an indication of His pursuit of us, because He loves us so: "If I go up to the heavens, you are there; if I make my bed in the depths, you are there. If I rise on the wings of the dawn, if I settle on the far side of the sea, even there your hand will guide me, your right hand will hold me fast" (Psalm 139:8–10, NIV).

I am in awe of the elaborate interweaving of lives, events, and circumstances God orchestrates to achieve His perfect will, and at the intricacy and complexity of His plans. His working all things together for good for multiple people may take time. It may result in delays about which we initially complain, but later praise Him when we awake to the wonder of His involvement. Through His signs and wonders we comprehend that God *is* with us all. They show us He understands and is ever ready to help us navigate and grow through our experiences in this complex, sometimes frightening, often difficult and challenging, but nonetheless magnificent world. They are evidence of what He has promised: "Never will I leave you; never will I forsake you" (Hebrews 13:5, NIV).

God's constant presence is a given and a fact. It is demonstrated throughout the Bible, from Genesis through Revelation. "We're already totally in the presence of God. What [may be] missing is awareness" (David Brenner). Whether you have that awareness or not, it may be that you are not reading this book by chance. Perhaps you are, or someone you know is, needing or seeking assurance, confirmation, or bolstered confidence of God's presence. He may have led or prompted you to read this book to give you precisely that. The stories by one or more of these writers may be meant to speak directly to your heart—to be a sign and a wonder for you.

My prayer is that this book will open your eyes to God's signs and wonders in your life, to things so inexplicable, grand, or extraordinary that they point directly to God's presence with and in you. As the star in the east was a sign and a wonder to the three wise men, leading them to Jesus, may this collection of real-life events that you hold in your hands lead you to Him.

———— ⋅ ✦ ⋅ ————

God knows how to wait,
dynamically; everybody else
is in a hurry. Some things
cannot be forced but they
must unfold, sending their
tendrils deep into the heart
of life, gathering strength and
power with the unfolding days.

—Howard Thurman, theologian

CHAPTER 1

Everyday Touches of the Divine

A Few Words
Can Change a Life

By Laura Bailey

Two years had passed since I left my career, trading in my
power pumps for yoga pants, becoming a stay-at-home mom
to my two young girls. But I was restless in that role; had I
made a mistake? Desperate for validation and purpose outside
my home, I began working part-time for my past employer.
I only worked a few hours a week from home, juggling sales
calls between changing diapers, playing with dolls, and taking
care of the never-ending laundry. At the end of the day,
I would plop down on the couch, spent after wrangling my
two young girls.

One day I was asked if I could attend a weeklong conference. Thinking this would be an opportunity to enjoy
the kid-free time, eat at adult-only restaurants, and get a full,
uninterrupted eight hours of sleep, I jumped at the chance.

A few months before the trip, I'd begun journaling reflections
based on that day's Bible reading. I felt a strong urge to write more
formally but quickly dismissed the notion. I wasn't a writer or a
seminarian; I was just a mom with small kids, scribbling thoughts
on paper. While at the conference, I had dinner with a gentleman
who had recently started a blog. He shared his experience and
asked if I'd ever considered writing one. Startled by his question,

I couldn't help but think this conversation was a prompting by God to begin publishing my words beyond my journal.

I explained that I'd begun writing down various thoughts and ideas for articles and devotions but was too embarrassed to share them with anyone else. My experience was in sales, I told him. I was not a writer. I didn't even know where to put all the commas. Upon further conversation, I discovered the young man was a believer and had grown up in the church his father pastored. Leaving dinner that night, one piece of advice stuck with me: "Just write and let God do the rest."

That was the problem. I wasn't used to letting God lead. I always had a plan of action, a road map for success; I wasn't great at

For our light and momentary troubles are achieving for us an eternal glory that far outweighs them all. So we fix our eyes not on what is seen, but on what is unseen, since what is seen is temporary, but what is unseen is eternal.

—2 CORINTHIANS 4:17–18 (NIV)

waiting on God. Still, I decided to walk out in faith and published my first blog post a few weeks after returning home from my business trip. For the first couple of months, my mom and a few friends were the only readers. But then I realized that the words weren't meant to change the world—they were meant to change me.

And so I kept blogging in addition to working part-time, mothering my girls, and taking care of our home. A few more months passed, and I was exhausted, trying to do it all. As I sat in my car waiting to pick up my daughter from preschool, tears began to form in the corners of my eyes.

I was in turmoil. I knew God wanted me to give up my part-time job, but pridefully, I just couldn't let it go. What will people think of me? What will I do all day? I begged God for more energy, for my youngest child to sleep through the night, and for long nap times where I could finally catch up on life and work. I wanted God to wave His magic wand and fix the mess I'd created from my desire to have it all. I was acting just like my toddler, arguing with God, thinking I knew better, and pitching a full-blown tantrum because I couldn't have it my way. "OK, fine, God. If you want me to stop working, then you will need to close the door," I screamed into the air. And the next day He did.

My boss called and told me I would need to either transition to full-time work or leave the company. I politely thanked her for the opportunity and turned in my resignation. I knew if I didn't walk away, I would be in direct disobedience to God. He had something different planned for my life. I just needed to move out of the way and let Him work.

> **Therefore, I urge you, brothers and sisters, in view of God's mercy, to offer your bodies as a living sacrifice, holy and pleasing to God—this is your true and proper worship.**
>
> **—ROMANS 12:1 (NIV)**

A few weeks later I found out we were having a third baby. I began writing more consistently with the extra time in my day. I signed up for a writer's conference and even submitted my work to various ministries and publications. As the months passed, I couldn't quench my appetite to know God's Word deeper. Although I'd grown up in the church, my faith was mediocre at best. I felt God leading me to seminary and enrolled in a women's Bible study program. For two years, I learned how to read my Bible, properly handle Scripture, and apply it to my life in a practical way. I listened to sermons while nursing my newborn. I wrote papers while bouncing a toddler on my lap. I read the Bible while rubbing my little girl's back before bedtime. There wasn't a lot of "me time" in those months, but God stretched and grew my faith radically. The Lord helped shift my perspective from temporal to eternal.

This world will feed us the lie that significance is found in a job title, a bank statement, social followers, or status. Not all kingdom assignments are glamorous, certainly not balancing motherhood and ministry, and those years were sleepless, chaotic, and required patience and perseverance. But by God's grace, He used the little time I offered to produce fruit in my life. I joined the writing team of an international women's ministry, wrote a book and a Bible study, and began leading a women's group at my church.

My life is not what I'd planned; it is better. I know that God used that one conversation at dinner on a business trip to change the trajectory of my life completely. I often think about those two conversations—one with my former colleague and another with my boss—and am amazed at the goodness, patience, and grace of God. I thought I had it all figured out, but God had a different plan for my life. He continues to direct my path, and His purpose will always prevail.

The Butterfly

By Dawn Damon

I shoved the last of my clothing into the Monos suitcase that was overflowing onto my cream silk bedspread, then tucked stray fabric in and zipped it up. I smiled at how "scripturally" I'd packed—everything pressed down, shaken together, running over (Luke 6:38). Preparing for my ministry trip to California had taken more time and planning than I'd scheduled. I'd received a special invitation to speak at a popular women's retreat, and I felt excited about the opportunity.

And a bit obsessive. I'd been preparing for weeks.

Had I remembered everything?

I went over my checklist one last time.

Four outfits? *Check.*

Noise machine for sleeping? *Check.*

Exercise gear? *Check.*

Makeup? *Check. No way I was forgetting that!*

Accessories? *Oh no! Had I packed coordinating jewels to complete my outfits?* I wasn't sure. *I'd better double-check,* I told myself.

I reopened my overstuffed suitcase and carefully patted around inside, feeling for my jewelry case while struggling to keep an avalanche of items from tumbling out. My fingers brushed the velvet pouch, just under my yoga pants. *Check.*

That's when I heard Him—the poignant whisper of the Holy Spirit.

You don't have every piece of jewelry you will need. Go back and get the ring I will show you.

The Lord was nudging me to pack something I wouldn't have otherwise thought of. This wasn't the first time God had spoken to me. Not too long ago, another whisper had come to me as God impressed upon me to call a friend I hadn't spoken to in weeks. When she answered her voice was fragile, and she was crying. Just moments before she'd received a call that her biopsy was positive—she had cancer.

I'd learned to listen and respond to God's messages.

"OK, Lord, which ring am I bringing?" I asked aloud as I walked to my vintage dresser and opened my ring case.

> **He will wipe every tear from their eyes. There will be no more death or mourning or crying or pain, for the old order of things has passed away.**
>
> **—REVELATION 21:4 (NIV)**

Bring the jeweled butterfly ring and give it to a woman I will show you.

Inwardly, the voice of the Holy Spirit gave me crystal-clear direction. My butterfly ring was chosen to grace the hand of someone special at the retreat, someone the Lord had taken extra care to set apart.

"The Butterfly," as I called it, was a special piece of jewelry I'd purchased from a rescue-mission boutique. This nonprofit ministry rescues and rehabilitates women who were once trafficked in the sex trade. Rescued women create these beautiful rings that declare their new beginnings, just like the butterfly.

I plucked the ring from where it nestled, tucked it inside a velvet pouch, walked back to my suitcase on the bed, and strategically placed the small jewelry bag back in my bulging suitcase. I felt a twinge of excitement as I anticipated the future gift giving.

I don't want to mess this up, Lord. How will I know who to give it to? What if I pick the wrong person?

I interrupted my thoughts and declared out loud, "Oh, Dawn, stop being silly." I realized that if I could sense God in *this* moment, I'd also hear His voice when the time was right.

My heart at rest, I grabbed my things and headed to the airport.

I arrived at the beautiful California conference center in the heart of the Redwoods, a spectacular and therapeutic setting for women to retreat with God. I enjoyed connecting with the precious ladies, laughing and chatting during the breaks, and speaking about freedom—stepping out of fear and insecurity to become the women God designed. I felt empowered and refreshed by our time together studying God's Word, but I still hadn't found the woman who was to receive the butterfly ring.

During the last three days of the conference, I kept the ring in my side pocket. But time was running out—the conference was ending, and I was presenting the last session. Still I heard nothing and started to wonder if I'd initially heard the Lord correctly.

I finished teaching the last session and, I invited the ladies to respond to any promptings they'd received from God by coming to the altar for prayer. Women poured down the aisle and flooded the altar. The Lord was moving in a gentle but powerful way, setting these women free from their fear.

Wilma, one of the attendees, was bowed over and crying, but not with joy. Her anguish was palatable. Wilma, a jovial, dimple-cheeked firecracker of a lady who dripped with enthusiasm, had crumpled to the floor. I hadn't discerned her pain earlier in the conference.

"Why, why, why?" Wilma agonized.

I wrapped my arms around her to comfort and pray for her, but I felt inadequate. "Lord," I whispered, "heal her heart."

Wilma wiped her eyes and turned her face toward me. Eyes that once danced with delight earlier in the week now looked like pools of bitter pain and confusion.

"Why, Dawn? Why don't I ever see butterflies?"

Her question staggered me.

What did she just say? Did she say butterflies? And what in the world does she mean?

"Can you explain, dear?" I muttered.

Through tears, Wilma poured out a mother's grief.

"My beautiful daughter Sophia was murdered. She was lured into drugs and addiction through an evil man she thought she loved. He trafficked Sophia and turned her into a sex slave. We could not rescue her in time. She's gone, forever, and all I have left is a grave."

By now we were both crying. "I am so sorry for your tragedy." I squeezed her closer as I spoke. "Speaking about her has to be incredibly painful for you."

"You have no idea, Dawn. I wouldn't wish this devastation on anyone."

I reached for Wilma's hand. She was right. I had no personal knowledge of this unspeakable heartache.

Lord, anoint my tongue and give me words to comfort Wilma.

I felt God's warm presence with us, and His reassurance reminded me that He *does* have personal knowledge of this kind of pain.

I squeezed Wilma's hand tightly. "Sweet Wilma, you asked why you don't see butterflies. Can you tell me more about that?" I tenderly probed. She winced again, as she returned once again to her tragic story.

"I have another daughter named Kayla. Kayla tells me that when she visits Sophia's grave, she always sees butterflies. Because Sophia loved butterflies, Kayla believes it's God's way of saying Sophia is with Him and she is happy. But when I go to visit Sophia, I see nothing. No butterflies. *Nothing.* Why doesn't God show me that my little girl is OK? Why?"

> ## The LORD is close to the brokenhearted and saves those who are crushed in spirit.
>
> —PSALM 34:18 (NIV)

Wilma put her hands over her face and sobbed. Not only was she grieving the loss of her daughter, but she was also experiencing the sting of perceived rejection from her Heavenly Father. I put my hands over my face and cried too. But not for the same reason.

I'd finally found *her.* The woman I'd been looking for was sitting next to me, praying for a butterfly! My mind raced, recounting all the details God had orchestrated for this very moment. He'd impressed me to buy a special ring, to say yes to a speaking invitation, to pack a specific item, to board a plane, and to meet a woman named Wilma and give her a butterfly ring made by women rescued from sex trafficking.

God, You're amazing. You love Wilma so much, You sent her a butterfly, special delivery. You care about every detail of our lives and keep a record of our human suffering.

I turned toward Wilma and quietly recited Psalm 56:8 (NLT): "You keep track of all my sorrows. You have collected all my tears in your bottle. You have recorded each one in your book."

GOD'S GIFT OF TASTE
— By Eryn Lynum —

MONARCH CATERPILLARS HAVE an incredible, and even lifesaving, sense of taste. Poisonous milkweed is the surprising snack of choice for the monarch. The plant threatens hungry creatures with its milky, latex sap that glues mouths shut upon eating. If this sap bleeds from a leaf a monarch caterpillar is snacking on, the creature halts its meal at once. It travels to the midrib of the plant and gnaws through its vein, severing the flow of toxic sap, making the leaves safe to enjoy. Similarly, God's Spirit guides His children in sensing toxicity in their lives and cutting it off at its source.

I opened Wilma's hand. "My sister, I have something for you. Actually, God your Heavenly Father has something for you."

Wilma looked at me through red, tear-stained eyes as I retrieved the carefully wrapped gem from my pocket. I slowly unfolded the colored tissue paper as I told Wilma every detail of my side of *her* story—the story I was honored to be part of.

"Wilma," I said as I placed the sparkling ring in her hand, "here is your butterfly. God loves you so much, He sent me to tell you He's holding Sophia. She's safe and happy."

Wilma gasped, then let out a shout of joy that still reverberates in my heart today.

"Oh, thank You, Jesus! You do love me. You really do!"

Wilma and I embraced, both of us awestruck by how God used us to do His extraordinary work and glorify Him.

Normandy Brother

By Dr. Marla Campbell

Sometimes what we perceive to be delays or chance meetings often serve as God's perfect timing in disguise. He uses such moments in our lives to set the stage for His divine appointments and life-changing moments. The ways that God has orchestrated and moved in my life has left me breathless at times. In one such instance, He took an ordinary woman and transported her across the Atlantic to kneel and pray on the immortal French Coast of Normandy—and under the most remarkable of circumstances.

As the director of the Prayer Connection for Europe, a branch of the larger nonprofit organization I worked for, I was invited by Irish friends I'd worked with previously to "cross the pond" and join them in a prayer circuit along the Normandy Coast. We had felt the pull to do this for over a year, but the COVID-19 pandemic had produced travel restrictions that prohibited me from even getting to Ireland to meet my friends, much less travel on to France. Then, seemingly overnight, both Ireland's and France's borders opened, making our prayer-focused trip possible.

Michael, from Belfast, Northern Ireland, met us in Dublin with his Range Rover. We—my three friends Michael, Ann, and Barry, and I—would embark on the nineteen-hour journey across the English Channel on the Irish ferry. Upon disembarking, our plan was to find a café first, since we knew we would be hungry. Little did we know our ferry would be a serendipitous hour late.

But when we stepped on shore and headed toward the village of Cherbourg where we would be staying, our attention was immediately diverted from finding a restaurant. Although we were walking among the crowd that had disembarked, as well as a growing group of locals, a hushed silence filled the air. Then our eyes fell upon what other people were noticing all around us—an astonishing number of tributes to and memorabilia from World War II. Members of our group silently drifted apart, each quietly pausing at various commemorative sites as they wandered. After a few moments, I spotted a small crowd gathering outdoors behind a low stone wall interrupted by a wooden gate. A nearby sign read *Ferme*, or *Closed*.

> **Things that we have heard and known, that our fathers have told us. We will not hide them from their children but tell to the coming generation the glorious deeds of the LORD, and his might, and the wonders that he has done.**
>
> —PSALM 78:3–4 (ESV)

I walked toward the wall and peered over the edge. An elderly man wearing a military cap was alone and walking slowly. American flags were being flown, so I assumed the lawn was being used for a private party. In addition to the man strolling the garden, others were seated at tables. As I paused to watch, a much younger man approached me.

"*Vous etes Americiane?*" I inquired.

"*Oui*," the young man replied. Both the older and younger men wore American Veterans of Foreign Wars caps, and a US flag flew over what appeared to be a luncheon.

"What's the event?" I asked the younger man.

He introduced himself as Andrew, a veteran of the wars in Iraq and Afghanistan and the author of a book titled *The Rifle.* "My engagement in those wars left me with PTSD. I was so depressed I didn't know if I could or even wanted to go on with my life. When I started thinking about the vets who were still living who had engaged in WWII and other legendary battles, I made an important connection.

"Men who fought in WWII are now in their nineties," he explained. "They lived another seventy-five-plus years after WWII, and frankly I was curious as to how they did it!"

Andrew continued, telling me how he was on a mission to learn from these vets. He searched the US, locating and meeting with several hundred WWII vets who agreed to meet and talk with him. The most profound moment during each conversation came when he placed a rifle in each soldier's hands, asking each veteran to let the rifle tell the stories of what they witnessed during the horrific battles. For most, the rifle became a symbol of healing. For many veterans, this moment was the first time they'd ever put words to their trauma and given it a voice. A time of healing ensued for each soldier, including Andrew, the young author.

I felt a lump in my throat as I thanked him for his service and for honoring these brave men. The older soldier had slowly come to stand alongside us. I thanked him, too, noting I would not have my freedom if not for courageous men like the two of them.

During this discourse, my three Irish friends joined and listened intently. I proceeded to ask the elder vet, "Sir, may I ask you your name and age, please?"

"My name is Bob. I'm ninety-five years old."

I took a deep breath and exhaled as I felt my eyes quickly fill. "My dad also fought in WWII and received a Purple Heart, but in the Pacific theater. His name is Bob, too, and he'd be the same age!"

My Irish friend Barry, who'd been standing with us, asked Bob, "What's your full name?"

"Robert White," the man replied.

Barry, pale now, stuttered a bit as his eyes grew wide.

As if in slow motion, I watched Barry's wife turn suddenly to both him and Bob, saying, "My husband's real name is Robert White too!"

"We have the same name! I'm from Ireland, and my father fought here when you did. He was captured by the Nazis and taken to a camp in Belgium. Later he made his escape to Le Havre, France. He hid under a train there when the fighting raged. Finally, he reached Dunkirk and was rescued."

By this time there were no dry eyes in our circle.

As we spoke, Bob's son joined us. "My dad never spoke of the war. When Andrew placed the rifle in Dad's hands, well, that was the first time we'd ever heard what really happened."

"May I pray for you?" I asked. Everyone nodded as the eight of us embraced. "Thank You, Jesus, for these brave men who fought for our freedom, willing to give their lives. Thank You, Jesus, for giving Your life 2,000 years ago so that we all have opportunity to receive Your gift of eternal freedom."

That day, the one-hour-late Irish ferry trip provided a serendipitous, God-ordained "chance meeting" that affected all of us. I was overwhelmed by the honor of watching this story unfold.

> **Remember the days of old; consider the years of many generations; ask your father, and he will show you, your elders, and they will tell you.**
>
> —DEUTERONOMY 32:7 (ESV)

After our time in Ireland, we continued up the Normandy Coast, stopping at each beachhead to thank God for those who sacrificed so much and praying that the God who sacrificed His Son would be known on the Normandy Coast and the entire continent.

Although this was not the first time a God moment impacted me profoundly, it reminded me how God uses ordinary people like me to remind others that He knows all of us by name. Even in the most perilous times, God is writing *His* story in history and in our lives individually.

Footprints in the Snow

By Shirley Gould

When an ice storm brought a blizzard to Jackson, Tennessee, shutting down the city, my preacher husband, JR, was home working on Sunday's sermon at our kitchen table. With a fire blazing in the fireplace and a pot of soup simmering on the stove, we were enjoying a cozy winter day. At eight months pregnant, I was doing laundry and light housework while our two daughters were laughing and playing in their rooms.

Given the icy conditions, I was surprised to hear a knock at the front door. I answered and found a lovely teenage girl standing there. She was bundled up in a gray coat and scarf with fur-lined snow boots. Long brown hair framed her pretty face and kind eyes. She smiled and asked if JR Gould lived at this address. I told her he did. I turned and called him to the door.

He greeted the young lady as she gave him an envelope. "I'm to give you this and take back your response." In the envelope was a check made out to JR for a large uneven amount. We were overwhelmed at the size of the gift. He told her to thank whoever had sent us such a blessing.

"Tell them it is an answer to prayer." She said she would relay the message.

My doctors had said I was infertile, so this pregnancy was a pleasant surprise. We weren't prepared for such an expense. Being uninsured, we had been praying for a financial miracle.

When a blood clot formed in my right foot two weeks later, the doctors decided to induce labor, delivering our third daughter two weeks early. The clot was lodged in a vein that could travel to my heart at any time. The doctors instructed me and my husband what to do if I had severe pain behind my knee. I was to drop to the ground, not move for any reason, and call 911. Since I was no longer pregnant, I was able to take blood thinners to begin dissolving the clot.

Our daughter weighed five pounds at birth and lost weight from there. She wasn't well. They released me from the hospital but couldn't release our baby. It is an excruciating experience for a mother to leave her sick newborn in the hospital and be taken out in a wheelchair with her arms empty. It's not what you envision when you've carried a baby within your body for months.

> **Be anxious for nothing, but in everything by prayer and supplication, with thanksgiving, let your requests be made known to God; and the peace of God, which surpasses all understanding, will guard your hearts and minds through Christ Jesus.**
>
> —PHILIPPIANS 4:6–7 (NKJV)

JR drove me home and helped me to bed, elevating my foot. As he was leaving to go to the church office, there was an urgent call from our pediatrician. Our baby's condition had worsened. She died three times and had to be given CPR to bring her back. They were preparing to transport her to a neo-natal unit at Methodist Hospital in Memphis, Tennessee. JR told them to wait for him. He hurried to the hospital and jumped into the ambulance as they were loading her incubator. As they rode with sirens blaring and lights flashing down Interstate 40, he watched her take every breath and prayed.

Upon arrival, they sent JR straight to the admissions desk and took our baby to the special unit for critically ill newborns. As he rode the elevator alone, the Enemy was screaming in his ear, "What are you going to do now, Preacher?"

JR answered, "There are a lot of things I don't know, but I *do* know My Redeemer lives and He is faithful."

Two days later, JR took my mother and me to Memphis to see our baby. She had needles and wires going in all directions and was surrounded by beeping monitors and nurses making notes on charts. Her tiny head was covered with wires that had been attached for a brain wave test. Her condition was consid-ered critical. I stood there and wept as I watched her fighting for life.

I remained in Memphis with dear ministry friends who took me to the hospital every day as my baby gained weight and strength. After an extended stay, her condition had stabi-lized somewhat; the doctors felt they'd done all they could, so my baby was transferred back to the hospital in Jackson via ambulance. I had to take CPR training for infants and be schooled on using her breathing and heart monitors before the doctors would consider releasing her into my care. One physi-cian informed me she would be a crib-death baby. He said, "I wouldn't get too attached."

With the monitors strapped to her tiny body, we took our baby home. It was a grand celebration to have our family together. The next leg of our journey had begun. During that first night, the alarms on her breathing monitor went off thirty-six times. We were exhausted, surviving on adrenaline and lots of prayers.

During this difficult time, the amount required for admittance for me and our baby at the hospital in Memphis and Jackson General Hospital twice proved impossible on our meager salary, but the check we'd been given covered those three amounts to the penny. A coincidence? I don't think so.

> **For your Father knows the things you have need of before you ask Him.**
>
> —MATTHEW 6:8 (NKJV)

Today, we continue to give the Lord praise for our baby's miracle of life. She is now grown, is happily married, and has three wonderful children of her own.

JR and I never discovered who gifted us the money. Being curious by nature, I went back to the front door to look for the car that had delivered the pretty girl to our home. But there was no car, no tire tracks. There were no indentations on the sidewalk. The snow was smooth, undisturbed. But there was a set of *footprints in the snow* on our front porch—and a miracle sent by God on a cold, wintry day.

The Knowing

By Jean Vaux

Welcomed sunlight bathed my skin on my morning walk
through the streets of our neighborhood. Sounds and smells of
spring provided a backdrop, as I reflected on the previous evening's long-distance phone conversation with my then thirty-
year-old daughter. She was concerned about her five-year-old
daughter playing by herself at kindergarten, rather than joining
in with the other kids.

"I feel so sad watching her play all alone. But she claims the
other kids are rowdy."

Silently, I empathized with how such a concern would
weigh on the heart of a parent of a firstborn child. Perhaps
my precious granddaughter had "inherited" her grandmother's
curiosity and sense of wonder. When she was six months of age,
I delighted in watching Hope pull and explore the grass in my
front yard like it was a new food or toy. At age three, our honey-
brown-haired cherub had pointed out her bedroom window,
asking if I could see the angels in the treetops! Oh, how I
wished I had her sight line!

As I continued my walk, I approached our neighborhood
elementary school. My attention was drawn to the corner of
the schoolyard nearest my path and the shape of another young
girl with honey-brown hair. A bundle of skinny arms and legs,
she was squatting, drawing in the dirt with a stick.

Oblivious to her kindergarten playmates, she lifted her stick "pencil" in the air, transforming it into a tightrope for the caterpillar balancing on its edge. Slowly, she stood and carefully carried it to a nearby flowering bush, helping the hijacked creature find safety among the leaves. She momentarily buried her nose in the blooms and inhaled deeply.

Then, the child jetted off to the swing set, skipping as high as her five-year-old legs would transport her. Taking flight on a swing, she lifted her legs higher and higher until she could lie back, her beautiful tresses dragging the ground, to take in her world upside down. With each return to the upright world, she squealed with delight.

> **The heavens declare the glory of God; the skies proclaim the work of his hands.**
>
> —PSALM 19:1 (NIV)

The scene transported me back to my childhood backyard. I was home in the afternoon from morning kindergarten while my older brothers were still in school. With the whole world of our backyard to myself, I put my senses to work. The specific designs and smells of flowers, the lifelike shapes in clouds, the musical sounds of birds and the whispered touch of gentle breezes on my cheeks all entertained me. My swing as my vehicle, I delighted in the world around me. Higher and higher I pumped my legs until I could lie all the way back, honey-brown tresses sweeping the upside-down earth, and sight spinning as I righted my body. I recited and embodied my mother's favorite childhood poem, "The Swing," by Robert

Louis Stevenson, which I made her tell me at bedtime so often that I knew it by heart:

> How do you like to go up in a swing,
>   Up in the air so blue?
> Oh, I do think it the pleasantest thing
>   Ever a child can do!
>
> Up in the air and over the wall,
>   Till I can see so wide,
> River and trees and cattle and all
>   Over the countryside—
>
> Till I look down on the garden green,
>   Down on the roof so brown—
> Up in the air I go flying again,
>   Up in the air and down!

But what happened in the next moment in my five-year-old universe will forever be ingrained in my mind. I had slowed my swing to a standstill. Suddenly, the thought exploded in my mind that this wonderful world must have been designed and created by someone even smarter than my engineer dad (who I thought was the smartest person on the planet).

Questions poured through my mind that day that still cause me to pause and marvel: *Why am I looking out of these eyes and hearing with these ears? Why am I feeling the breeze on this skin? Why am I inside this body and not inside someone else's? And why am I alive now, in this time, in this part of the world, and living with this family?*

Who made me, and why am I here?

I'd been taken to church since I was a tiny baby. I'd learned Bible stories in Sunday school, but this was my first "deep knowing" awareness of something much bigger and grander than anyone or anything on earth. Something, or someone, must rule over everything. In that moment, I first perceived the existence of God.

With that swing-inspired transformation, God became real to me in a place inside me I hadn't known before. At the age of five, apart from any human input, I became profoundly fascinated with a sense of divine design. As I pondered the mastery of a Creator and the mystery of where I fit into His world, I felt more alive than ever.

The new reality birthed an awareness of my lifeline and a personal connection to Jesus that transformed the Bible stories I'd colored on my Sunday school papers. I've relied on this lifeline over and over throughout my life when God has met me at various crossroads on my journey.

As I grew older, the closer I walked with God, the more I felt His presence. The more I sought His guidance, the greater the peace I felt in the good times and bad. Anytime I strayed, He was ready with a lifeline when I was ready to return. All I had to do was ask, believe, and respond to His nudges in "knowing" moments when I hear His voice.

"Knowing" has been a factor in achieving spiritual and personal milestones: deciding to trust that Jesus was who He claimed to be, bringing my husband and me together, foretelling the birth of my son. "Knowing" was present in career changes and choosing to direct writers' and speakers' workshops that spawned countless volumes and voices for God. His divine design is also threaded through my purpose and work today as a life design coach.

"Knowing" moments when I hear God's voice also happen in daily life when a "bird orchestra" wakes me up, when I find a prayed-for lost item, and after engaging with strangers who say they knew they were meant to cross paths with me.

Even in my sixth decade of life, I find the seat of a swing to be a comforting place when I need to inquire, "Who am I, and why am I here?" It's a touchpoint back to the lifeline tethered to my inquisitive, trusting, free-spirited self. Sailing on a swing helps me marvel at God's masterful design in creation and brings me to the "know-that-I-know" that links the earth with heaven and the present with eternity.

> **For since the creation of the world God's invisible qualities—his eternal power and divine nature—have been clearly seen.**
>
> **—ROMANS 1:20 (NIV)**

That morning as I watched the girl with honey-brown hair soar on the swing, I knew why Jesus greeted me with my childhood memory. He'd created a privileged opportunity for me to pass on His magnificent lifeline to my future generations.

That evening I called my daughter back and told her about my storied stroll past the school playground and the memory it had sparked. I encouraged her to not worry about *her* honey-brown-haired daughter when she's happy playing alone.

"Be thankful that she's creative and can find things to capture her interest independently. Important discoveries are often joyfully made in the 'classroom' of solitude. After all, Jesus told Martha that her sister Mary was doing the more

GOD'S GIFT OF HEARING
— By Eryn Lynum —

CHANGE IS OFTEN perceived from afar—a shifting of circumstances on the horizon. Sometimes it is welcome. Other times it induces hesitation or fear. With changing temperatures, aspen trees sing. This "quaking" of aspen is the result of a seasonal shift. A symphony rises as autumn breezes pass through a grove of aspen—their leaves dried and curled with time. In their song, one can hear praise to an unchanging God who guides His children through all of life's transitions. At every pivot and in each new season, God's children can declare with Psalm 40:3 (NIV), "He put a new song in my mouth, a hymn of praise to our God."

---

important thing to sit at His feet and learn from Him." With a laugh I added, "Besides, trust me on this—you'll be very happy if she doesn't want to be with the rowdy kids when she's a teenager!"

Three generations of my family were touched by my "chance" witness of the free-spirited honey-brown-haired girl on the playground. She was unaware of her audience or the part she played in a spiritual tapestry that could be titled, "Let the Children Come to Me." Over time and distance, God masterfully wove three little girls' lives together with the wonder-filled mystery that intrigues pure, open minds—of all ages.

Pearls of Comfort

By Lynn Brown

Four months before our son, Max, married his wonderful and
caring love, Britty, both Max and Britty lost their only remaining grandmas. Amid the joyous wedding plans, parties, and
bridal showers, there were two memorials, filling our families
with profound grief. It was a difficult and a beautiful time for
both families.

Britty had a very close relationship with her grandma Mary.
For most of Britty's life, she lived only a few miles away and
shared life's celebrations and milestones alongside her grandma.
Grandma Mary's ever-present faith planted the seed of God for
the entire family and served as an example to those who surrounded her. Britty clearly remembers her grandma made faith
a priority in her life.

After high school graduation, Britty went away to college
in Oregon. It was a new and exciting adventure for Britty
even though it took her far away from her close-knit family.
However, Britty made sure to find her way home for all major
holidays, special occasions, and summer breaks. When the time
came, Grandma Mary, who always made an extra effort for her
granddaughter, traveled the long distance necessary to attend
Britty's college graduation ceremony.

Eager to begin her career, Britty accepted a job that
landed her 580 miles from her family's home in Sacramento,

California. Having spent her last four years away from her loved ones, Britty grew homesick within months of working in an unfamiliar city. She moved back to her hometown, found a new job, and was once again near her family and her beloved grandma.

Within a few years, Britty and Max fell in love, and Grandma Mary came to know and love the young man her granddaughter adored. One Sunday afternoon, Britty and Max stopped by her grandparents' house to surprise them with news of their engagement. Britty recalls, "We stopped by unannounced. Grandma Mary and Grandpa were sitting in their living room. Grandma's face lit up when we walked into the house. When we told them we were engaged, they were thrilled with the news."

> **Follow my example, as I follow the example of Christ. I praise you for remembering me in everything and for holding to the traditions just as I passed them on to you.**
>
> —1 CORINTHIANS 11:1–2 (NIV)

Five months after Max and Britty announced their engagement, Grandma Mary learned she was terminally ill. She insistently told her doctor, "I'm planning to go to my granddaughter's wedding in October!" which was nine months away. Unfortunately, as the wedding day approached, Grandma Mary's health declined further. She tried desperately to hang on for Britty, but it soon became clear that the dream of having Grandma Mary at the wedding was going to be impossible. Nine weeks before her granddaughter's wedding, Grandma Mary died peacefully in her home surrounded by her loved ones.

The day after Grandma Mary died, Britty spent the afternoon at her parents' house. Having rushed home from their annual camping trip when they received a call that Grandma Mary was quickly failing, the family was mindlessly sorting through the camping gear they had haphazardly thrown into their cars. That evening Britty returned to her apartment and found that Max had done their laundry from the camping trip, stacking their clothes on top of the dryer. Sitting atop the neatly folded pile of clean laundry was a single pearl earring that Max had found when he pulled their clothes out of the washing machine.

Britty was confused at first. She didn't own any pearl earrings. "It took me a few minutes to process," she told me later, "but I quickly knew it was a gift from Grandma Mary. I sent a photo to my mom, then called her."

Surprised, Britty's mom commented, "Maybe she'll send you another one and you can wear them on your wedding day!"

A few days later, Britty had her first bridal gown fitting. In what would have been a shared and joyous occasion for Britty, her mom, and Grandma Mary, there were instead bittersweet moments filled with memories, laughter, and tears. Britty drove home from the fitting and managed to keep the sadness from creeping back by doing laundry. She had just finished her second load when a pearl earring inside the washing machine caught her eye. For a split second, Britty was baffled. She didn't know exactly how it got there, but she was certain she knew who had put it there. Britty sent her mom another photo and called her.

"I found another one!" she exclaimed.

This time Britty's mom suggested that maybe this pearl earring was one that Britty had just inherited from Max's grandma. Britty checked.

"No, those are still in their bag."

Britty's mom responded, "Grandma Mary is watching over you."

> **Ask and it will be given to you; seek and you will find; knock and the door will be opened to you. For everyone who asks receives; the one who seeks finds; and to the one who knocks, the door will be opened.**
>
> —MATTHEW 7:7–8 (NIV)

Weeks later, with just five days before the wedding, Britty went to the cemetery to visit Grandma Mary. On that warm, sunny day, she laid down on the lawn next to Grandma Mary's gravesite and began a conversation with the person she desperately missed. Britty told Grandma Mary she and Max had just received news that the offer they'd made on a house had been accepted.

"We're so excited. I wish you were here to see it," she said. Between tears Britty asked Grandma Mary for a special favor—to make her presence obvious on her wedding day, even though she would not physically be there.

The morning of the wedding, Britty's bridal party and immediate family gathered at the family home for brunch and mimosas. The atmosphere was joyous and festive as we all savored this much anticipated day. Britty was excited, and before we knew it, the time came to finish any last-minute touch-ups and get dressed. Britty's mom and I ducked into the master bedroom where our dresses were neatly hung. The bridal gown hung on the closet door, having just come back from alterations, and was secured in a long garment bag that covered the entire length of the gown. The bag was zipped up to the hanger and had been stapled at the bottom.

Britty's mom carefully unzipped and lowered the top of the garment bag to reveal the bodice, which had been care-fully stuffed with tissue paper. When she reached up to pull the tissue out of the bodice, she said, "Something fell. Something fell into the dress." Without removing any tissue, she carefully lowered her left hand into the bodice to retrieve whatever was resting inside the gown. When her hand emerged from the gown, she was holding a beautiful pearl earring. Britty's mom recognized it immediately. It was unique, with three pearls side by side, attached by thin threads of gold to a single pearl that was nestled in a golden cup. This had been one of Grandma Mary's earrings.

"How'd that get in there?" Britty's mom asked. Wide-eyed, she and I stared at each other. We knew.

Knowing the importance of this final and healing message, she hurriedly left the room to tell Britty. Through the power and grace of God, Grandma Mary was able to honor Britty's request and "make it obvious" she was there and would be with Britty on her wedding day.

Through a series of amazing surprises, God revealed His power and love for Grandma Mary, Britty, and the entire family.

Soul Connection

By Shelly Beach

Although I couldn't see or hear her, I sensed her presence behind me and felt the weight of her gaze on my back. I turned
in my chair. She stood outlined in the doorway as she did every
morning, her plush pink robe slightly askew.

"Hi, Mom. Do you need to go to the bathroom?" I glanced
at the clock on my desk. Five twenty a.m. *Nope. This is probably
it. She's probably done for the night.*

She took a few steps into my office and stood silently next
to my chair.

"You're going to get cold, Mom. Why don't we go to the
living room and cover up with a blanket and watch *I Love Lucy*
together? I'll make you cinnamon cottage cheese and applesauce on toast."

I gently tug Mom down the hallway, into the living room,
and settle her on the couch with a DVD of *I Love Lucy* while
I make toast with warm cinnamon applesauce and cottage
cheese. I can get back to my manuscript later…maybe when
Dad gets up.

My morning is marked by attempts to clean the house,
punctuated with activities to keep Mom focused and safe.
Dad has found a way to secure the exterior doors. Dan and
I live on a road with a fifty-five mile-per-hour speed limit,
and one moment of distraction or slip of our memory could

mean disaster. And then there are the stairs to the basement. We secured them, but I was never sure we remembered to lock everything correctly, store hazardous items out of Mom's reach, and keep small items put away. If we leave change, jewelry, or small items on the counters, Mom eats them.

It had been tough since I'd quit my job to care for our parents—first Dan's dad with Parkinson's disease and heart disease. His mental illness had come with an unexpected toll on our family. And we had nowhere to go to talk about the challenges we faced—and had chosen for our kids— with our decision to care for our parents.

> **My command is this: Love each other as I have loved you. Greater love has no one than this: to lay down one's life for one's friends.**
>
> **—JOHN 15:12–13 (NIV)**

As an outlet for processing, I turned to writing to use my experiences to try to help other caregivers. After I'd published several books, requests for radio interviews began coming in.

One afternoon my phone rang moments after I'd finished an interview with a Florida radio station. I was surprised when I picked up and discovered Rebecca (not her real name), the woman who'd just interviewed me, on the line.

"Hey, Shelly, I just thought of something and thought I should mention it to you. I'm also interviewing a man named Steve Siler today about caregiving. He's the founder and executive director of an organization called Music for the Soul. They use the power of songs and stories to create a bridge to hope and healing. Right now, Steve's working on a project for caregivers, and I believe he's looking for an advisor for the project."

I thanked Rebecca and hung up. *An advisor for a project on caregiving?* It certainly sounded interesting, but who on earth was Steve Siler, and what was Music for the Soul? I silently envisioned a garage band creating music I couldn't possibly endorse for any number of reasons, but I decided to keep an open mind and check out Steve Siler and his organization.

The next Sunday when I went to church, I asked a young man who worked with a Christian film production company if he happened to know Steve Siler. He said that he did and the company he worked for had produced some of Steve's music videos. Apparently, Steve had multiple awards for songwriting and production.

Steve called me within the week. He was working on a project called *Dignity* for caregivers, and I did, indeed, become his advisor for the songs and spoken pieces on that project. He titled and created a song that captured the content of my first caregiving book, *Precious Lord, Take My Hand*. And I was privileged to produce a study guide for the *Dignity* project. Working in various capacities as advisor for *Dignity* helped me process the trauma of caring for not only my parents, but also other dearly beloved friends during a compressed period of my life.

I soon became a board member for Music for the Soul and have had the opportunity to help shape projects on dozens of topics: child abuse, grief, prebirth child loss, military trauma, adoption, betrayal, body image, and many more. As a survivor of an assault by a serial rapist and the mother of a sexual abuse survivor, my work with Music for the Soul has become life-giving to me. Steve Siler has become one of my closest friends, and it is my delight to say that I am one of the most influential members of his board—not in terms of financial giving—but in networking and outreach. I cannot say enough about the positive influence that this nonprofit has in the world.

I do not believe in chance or luck. I believe the good in the world that reaps an eternal harvest in the lives of people comes from God. Rebecca called me back that day because God prompted her to, and she listened and followed through. Her simple act prompted me to talk to Steve and become involved with an organization that offers people hope in the name of Jesus.

> **So in Christ we, though many, form one body, and each member belongs to all the others.**
>
> **—ROMANS 12:5 (NIV)**

God brought Steve and Music for the Soul into my life at a time when I needed help processing the daily grief of losing my mother, directly after the grief of losing my father-in-law. I was his primary caregiver for over five years. And now, at this writing, Steve's father is slipping away to the ravages of Alzheimer's. I have walked that road before him and know the shadows before they are cast. It is my turn to help him walk through this valley. Our seemingly chance meeting was God's perfect timing. It has strengthened both of us and given us a newfound sense of purpose that has come with shared vision, shared ministry, and shared faith in a God who heals and offers hope to the world.

Blessed You Shall Be

By AJ Larry

So real is Deuteronomy 28:6 (NKJV) that declares, "Blessed *shall* you *be* when you come in, and blessed *shall* you *be* when you go out." The scripture embodies a time when my husband, John, and I decided to expand our childcare center. We'd always prayed that God would bless our daily comings and goings, but never had we experienced a more blatant and tangible expression of His blessing in our professional lives.

It all started in 1994 when we opened our home-based childcare business licensed for five children. I reduced my full-time job at our local women's hospital to part-time weekends and worked Monday through Friday operating our childcare business. John continued to work full time with GTE. A year later, I quit my part-time job at the hospital, and we invested in a small two-bedroom home that we converted into a childcare center—after some minor construction, plumbing, electrical repairs, and a special-use permit. The building itself was 680 square feet, with large oak and pecan trees providing shade on the three-quarter-acre lot. In August 1996 we opened the doors to Tender Times Childcare Center; we were licensed to provide childcare to fifteen full-time private and subsidized students. As the demand for childcare grew, so did our desire to meet the demand.

A year later, plans were drawn up to add a modular unit on the property to accommodate more full-time students.

We submitted a proposal for a contract with the Hillsborough
County Board of County Commissioners (BOCC) Head
Start Program and were granted the opportunity to provide
services to twenty Head Start students—immediately filling
all twenty of our modular-unit slots! We then added fifteen
after-schoolers. The business was looking promising as the year
1998 came to a close. After a few more years we sought to
expand our business again—
and we didn't have to look far.

Our childcare center's
property line was adjacent
to a large commercial concrete building that sat on the
west corner of our facility.
The building had once been
a pest control office with a
separate aluminum structure used for storage. John and I had
spoken occasionally about the property, and we knew that
a large childcare center would work perfectly in that space.
Nevertheless, affording such a massive structure would be an
obstacle, although we knew we served a big God who could
perform the impossible. So I made it a habit of stretching out
my hand and saying a prayer each morning as I passed the
large gray building before parking at our humble house that
had been converted into a childcare center. I prayed that God
would grant us favor.

On most days, the building and parking lot appeared des-
olate, but one Saturday John noticed a car in the parking lot.
Curious about what was going on, John decided to inquire
if the property was for sale or lease. When John entered the
building, he was greeted by a woman who informed him that

> **Blessed are the pure
> in heart, for they
> shall see God.**
>
> —MATTHEW 5:8 (ESV)

the pest control company was in transition and was relocating to another part of town. The woman handed John the contact information of the father and son who owned the property so he could inquire about the building.

John contacted the son (I'll call him Raymond), and Raymond arranged for us to meet. On the day of the appointment, we walked over to the property and Raymond gave us the grand tour that we had eagerly awaited. The space was massive— over 5,000 square feet—and we couldn't help envisioning how we would utilize every inch of the space. The reception area was spacious, and there were ample offices. The enormous safe would contain our confidential files and other storage items. The separate aluminum structure, which was over 1,600 square feet, could be completely gutted to become the dining facility.

After the tour, Raymond mentioned that his father was not in favor of moving the pest control business across town. He also said that the property was not for sale or lease, but that he'd let us know if things changed. Though disappointed, we focused our attention elsewhere.

Months passed, and we'd forgotten about our conversation with Raymond until a "For Sale" sign showed up on the property. *Did Raymond forget about us?* We felt a little slighted. John decided not to contact Raymond and instead contacted the Realtor listed on the sign to inquire about the listing price for the property. It was a price we could not afford.

One Wednesday evening as we prepared for Bible study, our home phone rang. It was Raymond. When John answered the phone, Raymond asked if we were still interested in the property. We told him we were. We had been on his mind— a lot, he'd said. He hadn't been able to sleep. He kept seeing our faces. He made John an offer that was $100,000 less than what the Realtor had quoted us. If we could qualify for the loan, then the building would be ours, he'd said. We went to church that night ecstatic about the offer. We knew God was up to something.

We hurried off to the bank the following morning to apply for the loan. Within three business days we received an approval—a stretch for a commercial loan. We rejoiced. On the day of closing, we arrived at the bank and took our seats around the huge oblong-shaped table, eager for the contract signing to get underway. Our banker was astonished.

"This never happens," he said, as he explained the "new" agreement. We'd heard for the first time that the property had been under contract with another buyer and that Raymond had chosen to pay a percentage to break that agreement—and sell to us at a lower price. John and I exchanged glances. Again, this had God's hands written all over it.

But seek first the kingdom of God and his righteousness, and all these things will be added to you.

—MATTHEW 6:33 (ESV)

The banker shook his head several times throughout the process as we signed all the legal forms. We could see him struggle as he discussed the terms with us. It was wonderful to see that God's handiwork was noticed by others even though they weren't sure of the reasoning. We knew, though, and it gave us an extra sense of gratitude and belonging. After our business was concluded with the bank, John and I finally had time to reflect on what God had done. We rejoiced in the

GOD'S GIFT OF HEARING

— By Eryn Lynum —

A RIVER OFFERS lyrical praise. It is a ballad composed of conditions and circumstances. Tones, tempo, and emphasis develop as the water gathers in pools, lets loose over rocky edges, and sways around bends. Every characteristic of the river's bottom, banks, and trajectory affects the river's song. Listening to its anthem, one can perceive how God utilizes every obstacle to shape the hearts of His children. Each challenge and change can lend to a stunning refrain of God's presence, power, and grace.

---

words found in Deuteronomy 10:21 (NIV): "He is the one you praise; he is your God, who performed for you those great and awesome wonders you saw with your own eyes."

We rejoiced all the way back to our humble childcare center that would later become our after-school clubhouse. And we reminisced about our humble beginnings from our home of five children to our new facility licensed for 109 children.

A Sign of Hope
By Mabel Ninan

When I pulled in to the church parking lot that Friday night, my heart was heavy. Before I left home, I'd read a text from my friend telling me she was pregnant. I lost count of the exclamation marks in her message. The reality that she was pregnant was truly unbelievable. We had been praying for months for God to bless us both with children, and God had answered our prayers. For her.

My thumbs typed a lightning-speed reply to my friend's text: "I'm happy for you! Praise God!" But anxiety and disappointment overshadowed my excitement. After years of praying for a second child, I had not yet become pregnant. *God, when will You answer my prayer?* pervaded my thoughts as months passed.

The desire for a second child grew stronger when my firstborn son turned three. My husband and I longed to become second-time parents, not wanting Ryan to grow up as an only child. Our relatives and friends often brought up the "only child syndrome," a common and popular but unproven belief that the lack of siblings made children selfish and socially awkward.

"When am I going to have a brother?" Ryan frequently asked us. Seeing other children playing with their siblings made him pine for a companion. Ryan was six years old, and I was getting along in age. I'd been waiting on God for a miracle baby for three years. I searched the Scripture to know God's will for me. I tried to decipher my dreams for some kind of coded message from God, a sign of hope I could hold on to. But He seemed to have gone silent on the issue.

That evening after reading my friend's text, I approached the church entrance with doubts and worries about my family's future circling my mind. Weary, I asked God to help put away my thoughts so I could focus on the task at hand. I volunteered to serve in children's ministry every Friday night. Even this was a reminder of the ache in my heart. Signing into children's church, I quickly glanced at my watch, which indicated that the children would start pouring through the doors within a few minutes. The volunteers had gathered for a time of prayer and planning.

> The LORD is good to those whose hope is in him, to the one who seeks him; it is good to wait quietly for the salvation of the LORD.
>
> —LAMENTATIONS 3:25–26 (NIV)

Soon the children started trickling in. They said goodbye to their parents, greeted the volunteers, and rushed in to the huge open space for a time of free play. The younger kids usually played with toy animals, while the older ones rolled hula hoops around the activity room. Some girls went to the costume chest and chose pretty dresses and tiaras to play dress-up. Other children played catch.

Amid the activity and noise, I noticed a little girl sitting by herself in the art corner, coloring. I knew Dolly, a six-year-old child who was a regular at our Friday evening children's church. Wondering why she was alone, I decided to offer her company. I pulled up a chair opposite her so I could see her face. Dolly had chosen a picture of a flowerpot that contained an elaborate web of flowers. She looked up at me and smiled, then continued coloring the petals of a flower red. We chatted for a bit about gardens and flowers as we matched the flowers with the right colors—the colors Dolly preferred. Within a few minutes another girl ran to our table, said hello to me, and picked up a coloring sheet.

"We're like sisters," Dolly announced. "That's Chloe. During the summer we spend a lot of time together."

"So, the two of you are friends?"

"We're cousins." Dolly stopped to pick up a green crayon for the stems and looked me in the eye. "Both of us don't have any siblings—you know, brothers or sisters."

Dolly's flowerpot bloomed with colorful, cheerful flowers. Only a single petal remained that required her attention. Though the room buzzed with noises of children running, laughing, and voices calling out to one another, an uncomfortable silence now inhabited the tiny art corner.

Suddenly, memories flashed through my mind of Ryan introducing his cousin to his friends at school as his sister. And when he drew pictures of our family, he always included my niece in them.

"My son is also an only child," I said softly, avoiding making eye contact with the girls. "God has a different plan for every family. Some have lots of children, but others have just one."

My throat had suddenly dried up. I wondered if God's plan for our family included only one child. There was no way of knowing. But I *did* know that the sorrow of not being able to hold another baby in my arms and the frustration of not know-ing God's plan for our family was increasing tension and frus-tration inside me.

I was weary of answering people's questions about when or if there would a sibling for Ryan.

Trust in the LORD with all your heart and lean not on your own understanding; in all your ways submit to him, and he will make your paths straight.

—PROVERBS 3:5–6 (NIV)

"It's all in God's hands," I'd say with a fake smile. I knew the words were true, but they didn't diminish the pain of celebrating my friends' baby showers. Praying for a second child had become routine and rote, sometimes half-hearted because I'd started to doubt God's faithfulness. Now, sitting with two six-year-old girls who had no brothers or sisters had brought my conflicted emotions to the surface. Yes, I did understand an only child's longing for a buddy at home with whom he or she could laugh, play, fight, and share secrets. A new cloud of despair settled over me.

But as I turned my attention to Dolly and her cousin, my perspective shifted. It was as if God brought me face to face with my heart so I could focus on Him. Blinking to restrain my tears, I managed to say, "God has a purpose for your families and mine. Because He loves us *so much*, we can trust that He always does what's best for us. God's plans for all His children are good."

The girls did not look up, but I knew they were listening while they worked on their art. Dolly picked up a marker and started to write on top of her sheet. I stared at the words she wrote in her six-year-old handwriting. A tingle ran through my veins. Goose bumps sprang up on my arms.

"God is faithful even when we are not."

Dolly looked up at me and grinned. "It's done."

I smiled, with tears of joy and a lightened heart. "It's beautiful," I whispered.

Right in front of my eyes. A sign of hope.

Through the words of a child, God reminded me of His unchanging love and faithfulness and transformed my attitude and my prayer life. I could trust Him to answer my prayers—whatever the answer—and meet all my needs in His time and in His Person.

God's love and perfect provision, both now and for the future, made my family complete.

A Home of Our Own

By Rebecca Borger

Every morning, the sun rises on my home, which is tucked into the woods. When I step outside, birdsong greets me. The light slants golden, tangles in the leaves and branches, and hits me full in the face bright and warm. It feels like grace. On windy days the sound that flows through the trees shelters me. The beauty is unrelenting and available whether I take notice or not. A visual and physical reminder of God's love and grace: abundant, generous, and constant. I close my eyes. I can't believe I live here.

It wasn't always this way.

I spent many years in a rental home, just twenty minutes north from my current home in Maryland. While that very rental home was itself a gift of God's grace, there were many things about life that challenged me to the depth of my soul. We had left a snug mountain home in the wild of Western North Carolina and by faith made a gutsy move to Maryland to be near extended family and necessary opportunities for our large and growing family. However, hardships followed us that we couldn't escape: health-related, economic, financial, social.

I couldn't see a way into a home of our own, even when different issues arose in our rental. So many times, all I could do was put everything into God's hand. Years followed. Many years of waiting. Many years of trusting in God when I could see no way out and no way in. Many years of walking in the dark. Day by day, waiting and hoping for a home of our own. Clinging to God.

In the spring of 2020, the constant tug I felt to move to a home of our own increased. After speaking with my husband, I took a step and called a mortgage broker to see if it might be possible for us to buy. The answer was a resounding no, but I had unknowingly spoken to someone totally unfamiliar with my state. Unaware of the laws and opportunities in Maryland, the broker gave me the wrong advice. Not knowing this, I shelved the desire once again and focused on other aspects of our life.

> **Trust in him at all times, O people; pour out your heart before him; God is a refuge for us.**
>
> —PSALM 62:8 (ESV)

A few months went by and circumstances within our rental home converged to push me again to try to find a home we could buy. This time I couldn't ignore the pressing urgency to move. Desperate, I began to research and search more carefully. It was August of 2020. The Lord was compelling me, and I couldn't give up, even though at times it seemed like there was nothing else to do.

I found our Realtor through the guiding hand of the Lord. I reached out about a listing online, and he replied swiftly. Soon we were visiting houses. He was a total gift from God: knowledgeable about the area, savvy yet honest, positive and kind, and protective of our interests.

The Realtor told us gently that what we were hoping for would be almost impossible. We would have to be very patient.

However, he never gave up. The market was madness. Houses were selling thousands of dollars above their asking prices. Buyers were paying sellers' closing costs. There was no way we could pay buyers' closing costs. We were actually hoping for help with ours.

More than four different mortgage companies told us that what we were hoping to do would never work, until we talked to another gift from God—a seasoned mortgage broker who had operated in our area for more than thirty years. He offered us a way, and we trusted his experience and recommendation, which aligned with the guidance we sensed from God. Daily, I wondered if I was crazy. Yet I couldn't stop the search.

One day in November, I saw a house way above our hoped-for purchase price. It had come on and off the market a couple times. In fact, it had been listed in June of 2020 and gone under contract twice. Both times failed. I looked at my husband and said, "Maybe this could work if…" He looked at me. It seemed impossible. With a wild leap of faith, we made arrangements with our Realtor to see it.

We found ourselves on a lovely, wooded lot. The driveway was slanted; the backyard reminded us of our mountain home, sloping down to the woods, with a stream winding through. Stepping inside, immediately we could feel the spaciousness of the layout. Our large family would fit. A lovely fragrance wafted throughout the home. It seemed to come from the very bones of the house. Good and pleasant.

I came to discover that the sellers were believers, and the presence of God was evident in every nook and cranny, from the Scripture verses tucked on painted rocks in the gardens to the artwork on their walls. They were praying for us. I felt stunned. I felt unworthy. Who deserves such goodness? Not me. Not us.

Reaching out to our mortgage broker, without any issue, we got approval for the needed price. Interest rates were so low that the monthly payment was within our means. We made an offer on the house. Adeptly, our Realtor navigated all aspects of the contract process for us. More than once, I knew we would not have known what to do without him. It turned out that the failed contracts were circumstantial for the potential buyers. Absolutely nothing was wrong with the house. The timing of it all took my breath away.

We bought the house, with so much goodness, yet unknown. We left our settlement with a check in hand—unheard of in the 2020–21 real estate market: God's utter provision and grace. We moved into the home of our hearts in February of 2021.

> **I believe that I shall look upon the goodness of the LORD in the land of the living! Wait for the LORD; be strong, and let your heart take courage; wait for the LORD!**
>
> **—PSALM 27:13–14 (ESV)**

With wonder, we realized that our house was listed at almost the exact time we first began our search. It went through two failed contracts through no fault of its own before we ever visited. The home and property contain so many details and unique touches that are personally meaningful to our family, in an intimate, God-breathed way. The Lord provided beyond what we could ask for or imagine in a situation that should have been impossible. With God, all things are possible.

GOD'S GIFT OF TASTE

— By Lawrence W. Wilson —

MANY PEOPLE HIKE to *see* the great outdoors. It's also possible to taste it. Blackberries make a delicious trail snack, and their dried roots are an herbal remedy for diarrhea. Roasted chicory roots are a coffee substitute. Dandelion leaves can be added to a salad. Young green pine needles make a tasty tea, high in vitamins A and C. The sense of taste need not be reserved for the dinner table. The flavor of God's creation is all around us.

Every season brings more grace before us. Personal, individualized grace like the beautiful butterfly bushes that line my driveway. I left my butterfly bushes in North Carolina in 2012. I woke up to purple blooms in the summer of 2021, more beautiful, more lush, and more filled with the delicate and gorgeous creatures than I could have asked for or imagined. And that's just a tiny glimpse. The grace here is like the ocean to me. I dip my cup, and it never ends. My heart wells with gratitude; this is our God. This is only the beginning.

I stood on the front step with my husband, and I thought of the life we have built and our beautiful home. There were times I felt like giving up; one very dark time, I wondered if we would make it. I wondered for years if we would ever again have a home of our own. I felt afraid, angry, uncertain, and alone during those years. All I could do was walk through each day, giving everything to God as best I could. I would have missed every beautiful thing stretching out before me but for God's intimate love and generous grace.

All God's Children

By JaneAnn Soetmelk

When my oldest daughter, Vicki, was selected to be a page in the Iowa House of Representatives, it was a blessing. The position offered a great opportunity for her to pursue her interest in politics, and it would be a strong entry on a future resume. However, it meant she'd miss out on activities with friends during her senior year of high school—not to mention that we'd miss having her at home.

Vicki would have to move to the capitol city of Des Moines. This would be quite a transition from life in a small town in rural Iowa, where we sometimes didn't lock the doors when we left home. She would also have to learn to drive in city traffic. I was relieved when we found an apartment within walking distance of the Capitol and within an hour's drive from Iowa State University, where she planned to attend classes in the fall. I resigned myself to the truth that this was an opportunity not to be missed. I waved goodbye to my daughter in January, knowing our lives would never be the same again.

When her term as a page ended in March, Vicki returned home to finish high school. However, she'd also just learned she was newly pregnant. My reactions were mixed when she told me. Immediately, I felt love for the baby and excited at the prospect of being a grandmother. I reached out to pat her tummy and told the baby, "I love you." Then I hugged my daughter and determined to protect Vicki as much as possible from the disappointment my mother had expressed when I became pregnant with my little girl. Although I had been five years older, engaged, and ready to graduate from University of Northern Iowa, my mother was deeply disappointed.

> **Children are a heritage from the LORD, offspring a reward from him.**
>
> —PSALM 127:3 (NIV)

Of course, I was concerned how the pregnancy would affect my daughter's graduation from high school, her plans to attend Iowa State University (ISU) in the fall, and her future career. Would she remain in good health and able to take a full load of classes? Would she miss out on memorable college experiences and opportunities? How could she possibly participate in extra-curricular activities? And what about extra expenses?

I was relieved to find out there would be no administrative problems involved in finishing high school and graduating as planned. However, her counselor awkwardly commented that "We haven't had many pregnant graduates in recent years." My discomfort must have been obvious because he quickly added, "Not that there haven't been pregnancies…"

Vicki's then-fiancé's parents and I agreed on having a wedding as soon as possible. Two weeks didn't allow much time to enjoy the planning process. The bride and groom had a small but lovely wedding and reception in the same church where her father and I were married and where my parents and grandparents had been lifelong members.

Shortly after graduation, Vicki and her husband moved near the ISU campus in Ames. Marriage made her eligible for a Pell Grant, which helped relieve their financial strain. Since she'd been living on her own in Des Moines, it was easier for me to adjust to her no longer living at home. I began walking in the mornings with a neighbor, the mother of one of Vicki's best friends. Several months later, she shared that her daughter was pregnant. Although she was worried about her daughter's future, her daughter had been adamant: "I love my baby's father, and I'm going to marry him." I felt privileged to be able to go to the hospital to visit my friend's new grandson when he was born.

A year or so later, another woman whose daughter had also become pregnant while in high school approached me. "I want to thank you. Your decision to support your daughter helped our family make the decision to support our daughter."

My heart warmed. My decision to help my daughter bring my first grandchild into the world had been driven by love. God graciously chose to use my story to bless other families with babies—eternal souls.

I was delighted when Vicki joined the ISU Marching Band Flag Line during her sophomore year. Her husband frequently took the baby to watch her practice and perform at halftime during football games. In her fourth year of college, Vicki was selected to serve as an intern for the Iowa Senate. Five years and three children after her marriage, Vicki graduated from Iowa State University. Soon after, she began working at ISU, where she is still employed.

All three of Vicki's children attended Iowa State, and she now has two more adopted children and three grandchildren of her own, with another grandchild on the way. She demonstrates a positive attitude despite life's ups and downs. Recently she had occasion to remind me, "Remember, Mom, it's all about mercy and forgiveness."

While at events around town, I often saw the sons born to the other two young mothers during their school years. But a third child was born to another of Vicki's classmates that I didn't meet until more than twenty years had passed.

> **See what great love the Father has lavished on us, that we should be called children of God! And that is what we are!**
>
> —1 JOHN 3:1 (NIV)

One winter day, I drove home to find my front yard piled with a foot of snow from the street to the house. I slowly high-stepped my way to the porch to get the snow shovel, then began to clear a path.

A young man exited the front door of the apartment across the street, strode over to me, then reached for my shovel. "May I help you?" he asked. "We just moved in this weekend."

I introduced myself and released my shovel as I asked his name. The last name stirred my memory. Could it be?

"What's your mother's name? And your dad's?" I could hardly believe his answer, especially since his family had been on my mind recently.

God?

I fought back a lump in my throat. "Your mom was in my daughter's class in school. She used to come to our house often with Vicki. Welcome to the neighborhood." I turned toward the house so he couldn't see my tears of joy. *God, thank You for allowing me to see firsthand another result of the ripple effect of choosing life.*

He refused to let me pay him and offered to shovel the sidewalk whenever it snowed. All winter long I came home to a cleared sidewalk. This young man came into my life at a time when I needed reassurance that God would take care of me after I had knee replacement surgery. Although my young angel moved away the following summer as unexpectedly as he'd appeared that winter, his willingness to help me with snow removal was a huge and unexpected blessing.

Meeting this young man was a well-timed confirmation of God's continued presence in our lives and in my life that winter. Through God's guidance in Vicki's decision to get married and have her baby, God influenced at least three other young mothers to do the same. At least three additional lives were saved.

God also addressed my concerns about her finances, experiences at college, and opportunities for her future. He blessed me with three wonderful grandchildren and more to come in the years following.

We may never know the impact we have on others, nor the long-term effects of our actions. But God knows. He is always with us, providing wisdom and discernment as we make each decision. We are all God's children, made on purpose for a purpose. God doesn't make mistakes. He even uses our mistakes to enable us to help others.

As long as I can help
somebody, inspire somebody,
encourage somebody, reach
down and uplift somebody,
I can serve the Lord.

—Sister Thea Bowman, scholar and speaker

CHAPTER 2

The Joy of
Helping Others

Step by Step

By Virginia Ruth

"I cannot stand that footprints poem," blurted one of the sweetest older women in my Bible study. The group of women sitting in a circle on folding chairs in the church basement simultaneously gasped and nervously giggled.

"Oh, Dottie, you don't mean that," said one of her friends.

"Yes I do," Dottie said emphatically. "I think it is misused in cheering up people who are struggling with burdens."

I was taken aback but didn't say anything. I knew what she meant, though. In some of my hardest journeys God didn't carry me but rather walked alongside, guiding each step. Sometimes He sent others to walk alongside me and help carry my burdens.

I thought about the times that I struggled to put one foot in front of the other. In a span of thirteen years, my husband and I were the caregivers, drivers, medical managers, and legal consultants to our respective parents. During those years we had periods of time when things moved along smoothly and other times when everything seemed to be thrown at us: health issues, family struggles, physical moves, even job changes.

"Who's taking care of us?" I would lament to my husband.

It was hard to know the next step in our caregiving. *Is this the time to have Dad stop driving? Will Mom agree to get neurological testing? How can we manage taking them to appointments and also get our office work done?*

"Heavenly Father, give us strength for today," we would pray during our morning devotions.

We found reassurance with God's Word. Many times we had to reclaim the promise in Proverbs 16:9 (NIV): "In their hearts, humans plan their course, but the LORD establishes their steps." As we journeyed through this caregiving time, we could plan for some things like appointments and medical decisions for the future, but we still needed God's help with our reactions to the day-to-day frustrations. We had to trust God with every step we took.

Bear one another's burdens.

—GALATIANS 6:2 (ESV)

I grumbled and complained but also felt sad and guilty. I knew the family members we were caring for weren't going to be with us for much longer. I wanted to enjoy the time that we had remaining. I tried leaning into Psalm 16:11 (NIV): "You make known to me the path of life; you will fill me with joy in your presence, with eternal pleasures at your right hand." Sometimes I felt God wasn't around helping me plan for us or our parents—and I certainly did not feel any joy.

Dear friends encouraged us during these rocky times with a timely email or phone call. They would drop off a meal, check in on our parents, help with our children, or send us a Bible verse that would remind us of God's promises in caring for our parents. Each offer of help furthered us along in our journey. When our parents died it was again our friends who came alongside us and helped with the heavy lifting of grief.

Shortly after our last parent's death, God's direction became clear. Our friend Tom was diagnosed with a debilitating disease and then a terminal cancer diagnosis. His wife, Martha, was bereft and overwhelmed at times.

"I am just about at my breaking point. I don't know if I can go forward," she would confide to me. It seemed as if every step she took would send her backward. Just when she would have a routine that fit her demanding work schedule and his medical needs, Tom's prognosis would deteriorate further, requiring more physical help from her. They would experience various home emergencies—flooding basement, hurricane winds, plumbing backups—all requiring time and attention that was in short supply and needed elsewhere. Then when she would get the difficulties straightened out, she would find financial obligations that her husband had forgotten to manage.

> **For God is not unjust so as to overlook your work and the love that you have shown for his name in serving the saints, as you still do.**
>
> —HEBREWS 6:10 (ESV)

Her words resonated with me—I had said something similar a couple of years earlier. While I longed to carry her through, I recognized that she had to take each step herself. She had to journey down this path. All I could do was try to relieve some of the burden or at least carry it with her so she knew she wasn't on this road alone.

The idea of walking together made me think about Jesus and His journey to the cross. Much as He asked God to take the cup from Him, Jesus still had to make that journey. No one could carry Him to the cross, yet Simon could and did carry the cross for Him when Jesus stumbled. They journeyed together up the hill to Calvary. The evening before, Jesus was not alone during his agonizing prayers to God. Even though Simon Peter and the other apostles fell asleep in Gethsemane, they were present with Jesus as He prayed for guidance during His final steps. Their spirit was willing to enter into and be present with Jesus during His dark night of the soul.

As Tom journeyed along, I felt like I was one of those who accompanied Jesus.

My husband and I were the contact people for Tom and Martha. We constantly heard "What can we do to help?" from people Tom had helped during his lifetime. Tom had walked alongside many people through their tough journeys and now that he and Martha were stumbling, others wanted to reciprocate.

Neighbors mowed the lawn. Colleagues helped with the practical matters of work and time off. Friends dropped off meals. Family did chores around the house. Acquaintances sat and chatted with Tom on the front porch.

"My yoke is easy and my burden is light," Jesus reminds us in Matthew 11:30 (NIV). God isn't necessarily burdening us. He knows journeying on this path is difficult. He makes it lighter for us if we stay connected to Him. He also makes it lighter by sending helpers and people to journey along with us.

As we learned with Tom as well as with our parents, we all are journeying to our mortal demise. Yet we need not be afraid or discouraged. We are not alone on the path. God is always present. While we might not see Him, He is with us, sharing our burdens and encouraging others to walk with us too. We might sometimes feel that there is only one set of footprints, but if we look closely, we will see the outline of others.

The Castle

By Dennis Gaxiola as told to Wanda Sanchez

Suddenly, it appeared directly in front of us—tall, isolated, with
a peculiar beauty: The Castle, aka Preston Correctional Facility.
My breath quickened, and a familiar, uncomfortable feeling hit
the pit of my stomach. I've always felt this way before I head
into prison, even though there is no place I'd rather be.

Our van is met by guards, and as we're led into the prison, I
feel a strong mix of emotions. Mostly, I feel humbled and grateful to be there. My thoughts are interrupted by the chaplain.

"Mr. Gaxiola," he said, pointing to the tower to the right
of the main building, "right there…That tower is where your
father did his time."

My eyes followed his finger as I looked up at the brick
structure my father had called home for several years, years that
had felt like a lifetime to me. A tsunami of emotion swept over
me, and a lump formed in my throat as I realized *once again* the
goodness of God that rescued my father, then me, from our bad
choices and turned both of our lives around.

That day, I was returning to the prison that so deeply
marked my father's life—and mine.

I turned toward the chaplain. "Hands down, my father
impacted my life more than anyone else. He was a bad dude,
a heroin addict who used his fists as much as his mouth
to communicate. He ended up in prison, where he was

introduced to Jesus, then went on to preach the gospel for over forty years."

The chaplain nodded. "I know your father's story. So do many of the guards and inmates here at The Castle. He did wonderful work for God, and you have good reasons to be proud of him."

I smiled, as precious memories of my father cascaded through my mind. It would make him happy to know that people remember him as a man whose life was truly transformed by Jesus.

"And because of my dad's strong faith," I said, "every day I try to be like him—living for Jesus and walking in my God-given purpose. I don't know if anyone here ever knew that when my mom became pregnant with me, her doctors were furious. They tried to persuade her to abort me. Repeatedly, they told her that if she tried to carry me to term, she'd probably die. But she refused. I wouldn't be here today if my mother hadn't had a strong faith in God."

The chaplain gently took my arm and directed me down the sidewalk. "If we could just walk as we continue talking,

> **The Spirit of the Sovereign LORD is on me, because the LORD has anointed me to proclaim good news to the poor. He has sent me to bind up the brokenhearted, to proclaim freedom for the captives and release from darkness for the prisoners.**
>
> **—ISAIAH 61:1 (NIV)**

Dennis. We don't want to keep a gymnasium of inmates waiting too long. They're really looking forward to hearing you."

I fell into step beside the chaplain, and we picked up the pace. I knew that my father's story—and mine—were coming full circle that day.

Only minutes before, as the Victory Outreach ministry van had pulled into The Castle parking lot in Ione, California, the mood among the other men in the van and I had noticeably shifted. Before opening the doors, we'd prayed. "Father, go before us. Prepare the hearts of the men to receive Your Word, and help them to see, hear, taste, and feel hope." The mood had been heavy with anticipation about what was going to happen over the next two hours behind the red-brick walls.

Keys clanged against heavy metal doors and confirmed that we'd entered the secure facility as we were led into a large auditorium. Thirty or so inmates in starched white T-shirts were moving in sync with one another as they set up chairs to accommodate the large group of men who would arrive shortly. My anticipation rose as I watched each row of chairs form. God Himself had prepared me for this moment.

I've had many proud moments in my life. I'm enormously proud of my family as the grandson of Reverend Sixto Sanchez, the son of Elias and Rachel Gaxiola, the husband of my lovely wife, Lorna, and the father of my gang of six children and five grandchildren (so far). I've also been blessed to serve my country in the military. My career in the military gave birth to my career as a comedian, and this career helped bring some of my wildest dreams to life. I opened for my favorite musical group, the legendary Earth, Wind and Fire. I worked with Jamie Foxx, Gabriel Iglesias, Paul Rodriguez, Gladys Knight, and many others, then watched my last *Dry Bar Comedy* show garner over

150 million social media hits. I still pinch myself to make sure it isn't a dream. But I am not a famous comedian. I am Lorna's husband, Elias and Rachel's son, and God's child.

And *this* moment at The Castle is the one I'd been anticipating the most in my life—to come into the prison where my father *lost* and then *found* his freedom and be afforded the privilege of sharing the gospel. *This* opportunity is the one I cannot think about without breaking down in tears of awe and gratitude.

"Thank You, Lord, for rescuing me. Now use me."

The loudspeaker crackled to life as the chaplain introduced me to the crowd. "Help me welcome to the stage one of the funniest men on the planet...the Bay Area's own *Dennis Gaxiola!*"

> **Continue to remember those in prison as if you were together with them in prison, and those who are mistreated as if you yourselves were suffering.**
>
> **—HEBREWS 13:3 (NIV)**

I bow my head, and over the hooting, hollering, and applause, I whisper my daily prayer..."Lord, please use me. I am honored and humbled to be here. Give the hopeless hope through our story. In Jesus's name..."

I bolt onto the stage and look out at the sea of faces staring back at me. These men are here to find hope. To find relief from pain and despair in laughter. To find the eternal answers in Jesus. The hope that changed my father's life.

Two hours later, I head back to the van with my team. My heart is bursting from the wonders of God.

"Are You the Library Lady?"

By Jennie Ivey

Heat waves shimmered off the asphalt as I pulled my car into
the parking lot of the one-room branch library I had just been
hired to manage. My predecessor had quit unexpectedly, and
I'd received only a couple of hours of training before filling
out my W-4 form and being handed the keys to the building.
Though I was an avid reader, I had only a vague idea of how
to run a library. As the only employee, I would need to handle every job. Get the computers up and running. Answer the
phone. Order books. Check them out and check them in.
Shelve them, too, which meant I needed at least a rudimentary
knowledge of the Dewey Decimal system.

If there was ever a time to pray, this was it. With hands still
gripping the steering wheel, I closed my eyes and bowed my
head. *Help me, Lord,* I whispered. It was all I had time for, and
I knew God could fill in the blanks. I grabbed my purse and
my lunch bag and scooted out of the car, my head so full of
questions that I didn't notice the little girl standing next to the
library entrance until she spoke.

"Hey," she said, as I fumbled in my pocket for the keys. "Are
you the new library lady?"

"I am," I told her. "Who are you?"

"Kaylee," she said. "And I just turned ten."

Hmm, I thought. Kaylee was certainly the smallest ten-year-old I'd ever seen. But it was clear she was old enough to read, for she had obviously noted the sign that said, "Children Younger than Ten Must Be Accompanied by an Adult."

I pushed the door open and flipped on the light switch. "Come on in here where it's cool, Kaylee," I said. "Let's see if we can find you some good books." Five minutes later, her arms loaded with Dr. Seuss and Amelia Bedelia and Curious George, Kaylee settled into the yellow beanbag chair in the corner of the library and began to read.

> **Whatever you do, work at it with all your heart.**
>
> —COLOSSIANS 3:23 (NIV)

I was booting up the computers when in walked a woman who looked and smelled as though she had not bathed in quite a while.

"I'm here to use the Internet," she said. She signed her name, Ada, in the logbook and settled down in front of one of the computers, which was positioned so that I could see the screen from the checkout desk. For the next two hours, Ada scrolled silently through Facebook. Then, without a word, she logged off and left.

Not long before closing time, the library door slowly opened and an elderly man leaning heavily on his walker entered. He made his way to the checkout desk and plopped a large-print Western down in front of me.

"This book didn't have a single cow in it!" he said, scowling.

"Excuse me?"

He leaned toward me. "Why would I want to read a Western with no cows?"

I looked at the book's cover, which pictured three mounted cowboys, lassos at the ready, pursuing a herd of cattle across a cactus-dotted landscape. I shrugged.

"I guess whoever designed the cover didn't read the book."

The man smiled just a little. "I'm Calvin Appling," he said. "Who are you?"

I introduced myself and walked with him to the shelf that held the large-print books. Skipping the romance section, I pulled out several Westerns and read the blurbs on the back covers aloud. If there was no mention of a roundup or rodeo or cattle drive, I reshelved it. Mr. Appling chose one of the books I'd laid out and handed me his library card.

"I'll be back next week for another one, young lady," he said, giving me a wink. "I'm obliged for your help."

Thus ended my first day on the job. The days and weeks that followed weren't all that different, at least on the surface. But as time passed, I learned more and more about the people who frequented this little library. Kaylee, who—as I suspected—was seven years old, not ten, was being raised by a single mom who had no one to watch her when she went to work. Ada lived in a run-down mobile home with a broken water heater. Mr. Appling had recently lost the wife to whom he'd been married for seventy-one years.

There were others too. Toby, the six-foot-six developmentally disabled man who came in once a week to dust the high shelves for me. Sheila, who tried unsuccessfully to hide her tiny dog in the same canvas tote bag where she kept her library books. (I pretended not to notice Sparky, even when he barked.) Brad, the sheriff's deputy who simply needed a quiet place to sit and decompress when his patrol duties were over.

The Dewey Decimal system was only the beginning of what I learned when I became the library lady. My most important lesson? You can be the hands and feet of Jesus in most any situation if you'll just keep your eyes and ears open. Sometimes it's as simple as a peanut butter sandwich in a brown paper bag for a little girl. Toiletries and clean towels in the restroom for someone living in squalor. A monthly book order of real cowboy literature for a lonely senior citizen.

> **We have sworn friendship with each other.**
>
> —1 SAMUEL 20:42 (NIV)

"Help me, Lord," I had whispered my first day on the job. I never quit whispering that prayer, even after I retired. I hold fast to the hope that the patrons at my dear little library saw God's loving presence in me, just as I saw Him shining in each of them.

Gifted to Give

By Becky Hofstad

In the bright light of our third morning in Haiti, perspiration inched down my back. As our short-term mission team walked through the concrete Missionaries of Charity campus, we noticed new structures with exposed rebar alongside other spaces where the rubble had yet to be cleared away. The destruction left in the wake of a 6.9 magnitude earthquake was still visible everywhere two years after the event. The entrance to our destination was tucked away in a section that had not been damaged, but was dark and cramped, almost forbidding.

We passed through the rickety screen door and were ushered into a large room filled with cribs. Six were placed end to end, four rows deep. These were not the full-size, luxurious cribs we have back home. They were only slightly larger than the tiny patients they housed. The odor of too much time spent in the same linens enveloped us. We advanced single file down an aisle between two rows of cribs, our arms brushing their frames. A couple of nurses scurried around murmuring in Creole. My stomach clenched. The need was too great, and we were too few.

I quickly moved through a doorway into a smaller room with fewer children, feeling some emotional relief. There, a baby with an IV lay in the center of the room. He was not much larger than his skeleton's bones, which were in plain view. He seemed too delicate to touch.

My husband, Mike, must have gone in another direction, but our teammate Alli had followed me into the room. We turned our attention to a couple of boys, crib neighbors across the aisle. They looked to be around two and a half but were likely older than their immature bodies suggested. Malnutrition and disease had already taken a double toll.

I stood next to the crib of the boy wearing a dark-blue T-shirt, while Alli focused her attention on the boy in the corner of the room. The only thing resembling toys were a couple of plastic teething rings in bright colors scattered in a few of the cribs. My boy kept his vacant gaze on the floor, his head of dark curls

> **A spiritual gift is given to each of us so we can help each other.**
>
> —1 CORINTHIANS 12:7 (NLT)

turned away from me. His rejection wasn't a judgment of my lack of skill in engaging young children, though he would have been accurate. No, he'd already learned not to open himself up to the fleeting attention of strangers. We might offer what he so desperately needed, but we would desert him quickly. I tried playing peekaboo, singing, attracting his attention with a teething ring, all to no avail. I went to touch his arm, intending to pick him up, but he pushed me away. I wondered if it was a test. "Keep trying so that I'll know you really care," I sensed him saying.

After what felt like a long struggle of trying to break through this boy's tough exterior, Mike reappeared. Alli and I described our failure to draw any engagement, much less a smile, from the boy, though there had been occasional stolen glances to see if we'd given up yet.

My husband was wearing his Gilligan hat, his intense eyes visible and focused on our young friend. Within seconds, there was interest. A series of games quickly followed. The toddler played with the hat, and then put the hat on Mike's head—upside down. Peekaboo, which I had tried earlier, followed. The boy giggled, saliva gurgling out of his mouth as he threw the teething ring into the hat. My husband's good-natured grin, the one that had captivated me years ago, communicated his mutual delight to the boy. Before long there were high fives and fist bumps all around, even for those of us he'd previously pushed away.

Had the boy sensed Mike's experienced ease with kids? Or his intuitive playfulness? Whatever it was, my husband was just the right person to draw the young boy into our small community that day. I was thankful to see how the joy in the room had become contagious. Other children perked up. The baby in the center of the room with the IV was now sitting up in his crib, and I thought I spotted the trace of a smile on his face.

> **If your gift is to encourage others, be encouraging. If it is giving, give generously. If God has given you leadership ability, take the responsibility seriously. And if you have a gift for showing kindness to others, do it gladly.**
>
> **—ROMANS 12:8 (NLT)**

GOD'S GIFT OF TOUCH

— By Eryn Lynum —

WARMTH FROM A fire is not only comforting; it is also insightful. Fire's heat is the product of consumption. It consumes fuel, simultaneously producing warmth. Hebrews 12:29 says, "God is a consuming fire." Backing up a few verses lends more context, painting a picture of a God who burns up everything temporal, making room for a kingdom that cannot be shaken. Devouring distractions, God produces the warmth of His presence and illumination from His Spirit. The warm crackle of a campfire or the dancing flicker of a candle serves as reminders of God's constant acts of consuming and producing.

Mike told me later that as he took in the scene of so many kids in need of attention, he prayed silently that God would show him what to do. He had no idea how he was going to be of any help to these sick children.

During these missions experiences, Mike and I never know when we'll be just the right person to bring what is needed. Often, we don't even know the impact we've had on someone else. Isn't it just like God to gift us with uniqueness and then use it to show His love to someone who needs it? The gifts He gives us get regifted to others through us.

We left Haiti knowing that we would have adopted any one of those kids. They had struggles, but they responded to love. God opened our hearts that day in that hospital room. Six months later we learned of a girl in Liberia with special needs. She's now been our daughter for eight years.

Hope toward Life

By Elsa Colopy

It shocked me when I found out that a young man I'd known for years was struggling with suicidal thoughts. It scared me. He had so much to offer, so much future ahead, and it was unthinkable to me that he would consider ending it all. My heart broke. I didn't know what I could do, but I knew I had to do something. I wrote a letter and shared it on my social media accounts. It was a heartfelt cry to those fighting depression, a plea for them to reconsider life, hope, and a future.

I lived in Colorado Springs, and my brother was interim pastoring at a church in Iowa. One of his volunteer staff read the letter and invited me to speak and share my heart at a suicide prevention event. After a spate of suicides in their community, this young, passionate mom wanted to reach the hurting teens in her community. Over 150 teens and volunteers attended and many were deeply touched by the music, skits, and speakers. After the impactful evening, I sat with my sister-in-law, who told me, "You could do this in your city too."

No, I couldn't.

At least that's what I thought before I prayed about it. Sure, as a freelance author and speaker, I'd been speaking at retreats and conferences of all kinds for twenty years, but coordinating my own event? While raising four little ones? Surely God wouldn't ask me to do something so big, so out of my reach.

A few weeks later I traveled to Oregon to speak at an adoption conference. Since adopting four little ones, my travel had lightened a bit, but my husband still graciously supported opportunities to communicate God's goodness through conferences and retreats. While there I prayed about organizing my own suicide prevention event.

God, do You want me to put on an event in Colorado Springs? The topic was heavy on my mind when I dropped my luggage back off at the airport to head home from Oregon. When I retrieved my bag at the Denver airport, I noticed a beaded flag pinned onto the

> **The LORD is God, and he has made his light shine on us.**
>
> —PSALM 118:27 (NIV)

baggage tag. What on earth? I looked closer and didn't know what it meant, so I looked it up online. It was the same ribbon used to raise awareness for suicide prevention.

Well then.

Just in case it was a coincidence, I met with a dear friend a few days later and invited her to pray. Would God call me to do this? Suddenly my phone pinged. Normally I have the sound off. I glanced down to see a headline flash on my screen. It was from the *New York Times*. "So many suicides. We need your help." I looked up at my friend with my eyes wide. "I think God is calling me to do this."

From TV commercials to music to even more headlines, God confirmed over and over His very specific calling. I was to put together a suicide-prevention event for my community. I knew it wasn't to be an informative conference. I wanted this event to inspire and encourage teens toward hope. I wanted to use the arts to remind them of the beauty that surrounds us. I wanted those who'd struggled with depression to share their stories to remind teens of the redemption that is possible.

I started by going to my local church and asking if their campus would host the event. I went to my community group and invited people to volunteer to put it all together. We had a rag-tag team of five members, sometimes seven, sometimes three. We met and talked about agenda, marketing, and practical resources that would help teens who were struggling.

> **May the God of hope fill you with all joy and peace as you trust in him, so that you may overflow with hope by the power of the Holy Spirit.**
>
> —ROMANS 15:13 (NIV)

A thousand things went wrong. Musicians committed and then backed out. Speakers signed on with great enthusiasm only to never return my calls later on. Volunteers dropped off the map and disappeared. Even on the night of the event, one of our food trucks broke down on the way to the venue.

But a thousand things went right. God prompted hearts of the most unlikely and beautiful souls. A neighbor coordinated a multitude of therapy dogs for the evening. Another neighbor committed to doing a photo booth. A show choir heard about the event and signed on to sing—they were one of the best-known high school choirs in the area. Two young dancers volunteered their gifting to do an incredibly moving dance telling a story of love and loss and hope. Police officers volunteered their time and counselors made themselves available to help anyone who might need to talk. Local businesses contributed gift cards for our giveaways, things that would allow teens to get out and about to connect. Coffee for two. Skydiving for four. Putt-putt golf for three. Whatever allowed for personal connection—those were the items we gave away.

We called the event "Light up the Dark" because we wanted teens to know they were born to light up the dark. We wanted this event to light up the dark—and we wanted to point teens to the only One who could truly light up their dark—Jesus.

The night came. I hadn't required advance registration because I wanted anyone who wanted to come to do so. We let local news stations know about the event and they put it on the news. And we waited.

The time came for people to arrive. We were set and ready to roll. One car pulled into the parking lot, then another… and another and another. The food trucks had lines, the tables were full, the conversation filled the quiet of the early evening. After food, the teens entered the auditorium. Music, drama, teaching, giveaways…and at the end a surprise. We played the song "One More Light" by Linkin Park. The chorus goes like this:

If they say
Who cares if one more light goes out
In a sky of a million stars
It flickers, flickers
Who cares when someone's time runs out
If a moment is all we are
We're quicker, quicker
Who cares if one more light goes out?
Well I do…

As the words "Well I do…" played, people from the community planted throughout the audience stood up. Each held up a sign. "I do." "I care." "You matter." "Don't let your light go out." "We need you."

The moment was powerful and beautiful—and as the students filed out of the building and drove off with their parents, they encountered a whole other slew of people from the community lining the streets with similar signs lit up by flashlights. "We love you." "You matter." "You belong." "You are loved."

> May your
> unfailing love be
> with us, LORD,
> even as we put
> our hope in you.
>
> —PSALM 33:22 (NIV)

After the event I stood with my group of volunteers. Over 450 teens had attended our evening. They left with giveaways in hand, a backpack full of resources to connect them with the community, and hope.

I was in awe of what God had done. It was so much bigger than I could do myself. It was only God who could have orchestrated such a lovefest for hurting teens. And some of the most impacted? The fifty show-choir participants who had volunteered their time. They left the venue, many in tears because of the love God poured out to them through the dance, the speakers, the volunteers. Many of them hadn't darkened the doors of a church for years, if ever. But in serving hurting teens in the community, they had been ministered to and loved on as well.

Only God is big enough as to not only love the hurting and broken beyond our doors, but to also love those who put themselves out there to serve.

So big, so beautiful—our God who lights up the dark.

Unexpected Gifts

By Patty McClurg

The doorbell rang, startling me from my nap. I opened the door, surprised to find a teenage girl standing on the porch. Blond hair framed a face accented by heavy makeup. Jeans clung to her thighs, and her thin shirt offered no protection from the chilly night air.

"Remember me?" Her voice was uncertain yet hopeful.

Clueless, I stammered something vague.

"Annie invited me to dinner once when you were helping her," she prompted.

Sara? Unsure, I hesitated.

"Sara. My mom threw me outta the house tonight and reported me as a runaway. Can I stay here?" Her eyes were pleading.

Lord, I barely know her!

Besides, I was pregnant, my placenta had partially torn from my uterus, and my doctor had ordered bed rest and no stress.

Anxiety would threaten my baby. Even our two-year-old was sent to childcare so I could rest. My husband was working *and* playing Mr. Mom. A feeling of being overwhelmed had long ago overtaken me.

I can't say no, but I can't keep her!

I silently prayed and moved her to the couch, where we'd be more comfortable. But Sara still looked nervous and unsure. I laid my hand gently on her arm.

"Honey, if your mom's reported you as a runaway, I'm required to tell the police you're here."

Surprisingly, she said she understood, and I hurried for the phone in the kitchen.

The officer who answered explained an option called "Equal Ground," an overnight shelter for teens that relied on the condition that parental dialogue is attempted the next day. With Sara's consent to those conditions, an officer took her to a shelter for the night.

Later, I stared at the ceiling, praying.

God, protect her. Help her hear You and sense Your presence. Help her see that she's profoundly loved by a perfect Father.

Early the next day, as I sat at the tiny built-in desk in our kitchen, Equal Ground called to tell me they'd called Sara's mother, who had refused dialogue. My heart broke with fresh pain.

> **Keep on loving one another as brothers and sisters. Do not forget to show hospitality to strangers, for by doing so some people have shown hospitality to angels without knowing it.**
>
> —HEBREWS 13:1–2 (NIV)

"What now?" I asked the social worker, as I searched for a pen to jot down their plan.

"Sara wants to stay with you."

My hand froze. "H-How long?" I stammered. *Maybe a week or two, while they find her a home?*

"Two to three years," the social worker answered.

I sucked in my breath. How could I possibly care for a teenager? I could barely care for my own family, let alone a runaway teen.

God, what am I supposed to do?

"I'm sorry, I can't," I stammered as I poured out my reasons, desperately hoping for absolution from the person listening.

Moments later I hung up, and with shaking hands, called my husband, Lynn, at work.

"The court called," I sobbed. "Sara's mom refused reconciliation, and Sara asked to live with us—for two or three years! I said no, and now I feel terrible."

"Then call back and tell them we will take her," Lynn replied calmly.

So, I did, shaking. When the police brought Sara back, Lynn and I gathered with her in the living room. I told her we had little to offer. I was on work leave. We couldn't afford to buy her new clothes. I was on bed rest and couldn't physically help her. We were stressed because of my high-risk pregnancy. We were planning to move, so our house was for sale. She'd have to leave her high school and friends.

When I finished, Sara told us why, at fifteen, she'd gone for counseling and decided if her mother threw her out of the house again, she'd leave for good. She realized she didn't know enough about life to succeed as an emancipated minor. She knew she needed mentors to teach her to function as a successful adult. She wanted to move away from unsafe, chaotic home and school environments.

Lynn and I recognized Sara's unique sense of purpose. Weeks later, she told us she'd often sat in her basement bedroom, looking out her small window at the stars, knowing God had to exist. But did He see her? Did He care about her, and would He provide for her when her mom threw her out again?

The horrible night when Sara walked away from the house she'd called home, she asked God where she should go. And He'd answered.

He'd given Sara a memory of having dinner at our house when her friend Annie had lived with us. Sara had never experienced anything like that—a family having fun together and a home that felt peaceful. Those simple qualities had imprinted on her memory, and after leaving her mother's house and walking through the cold night, she ended up on our doorstep.

> # No one should seek their own good, but the good of others.
>
> —1 CORINTHIANS 10:24 (NIV)

After probate court granted us temporary guardianship, we welcomed Sara home. She lived with us for three years and became family. We helped her integrate honesty, gratitude, and obedience into her life. She participated in our Christ-centered lifestyle, shared household work, applied herself diligently in school, and earned her own income.

However, like many trauma survivors, Sara was often ambushed by triggers. One common trigger is seeing someone who resembles an abuser. This stimulates the brain to replay past negative voices (lies) into self-talk: *Nothing will ever change; I might as well end it all.*

One day at school, Sara was triggered, and when she came home, I wasn't there, which escalated her anxiety. Later, in the hospital, she explained what happened as I sat beside her bed. Tears streamed down her face.

"After I saw someone who looked like him, the voices in my head wouldn't stop. All the old feelings came back. I didn't know what to do. They were saying my life would never get better and that killing myself would stop the pain."

Sara reached up and swept away tears with a tissue I'd given her. I stood and pulled her into a hug.

"I'm so sorry," she sobbed into my neck. "I know what I did wasn't right. I just wanted to stop the voices. They torture me." She squeezed me harder. "I want to get better, but I don't know what to do."

Slowly, I pulled away and wiped her tear-streaked face. "God feels every trauma and betrayal, and He hears the voices that torment you. Your pain is His pain. He wants to free you from these lies."

I left Sara with a teddy bear and assured her she still had a home with us, and we would keep her in prayer. When I returned the next day to take her home, her face was beaming. "I think God sent an angel to me. I woke up this morning and a strange woman was sitting on my bed. Somehow, she knew everything about my life. She told me she understood my pain and my life wouldn't always be like this. Then she left. I asked the nurses about her, but no one had seen her."

Sara's eyes widened. "I *know* it was an angel. She told me I'd be OK because God was with me and watching over me because I was His child. When she left, my fear was gone."

I delighted with her, and soon Sara gave her life to God and began a personal relationship with Him that radically shifted the trajectory of her life. Her commitment, however, didn't release her from the fallout of a broken life, but she faithfully trusted God during tough times.

Becoming part of Sara's story was God's gift to our family. Sara taught me how to accept what's real, not a tale I create with a happy ending. She also taught me to *choose* gratitude,

GOD'S GIFT OF SIGHT
— By Tez Brooks —

THERE'S MORE TO sight than what man can view with the human eye. Spiritual sight is much more critical. John 3:3 says that unless one is born again, he cannot see the kingdom of God. That's called spiritual blindness, according to Ephesians 4:17–18, and it leads to eternal separation from God. But if men or women keep their eyes on Jesus, Hebrews 12:1–3 says that people can set aside sins that easily entangle and run the race set before them with endurance. The body's literal eyesight is temporary, lasting only until this life is over—but spiritual vision is eternal.

no matter my circumstances. Additionally, Sara showed me that to accept others, I had to first accept myself. As a thirty-year-old attempting to parent a teen, my insight on life was limited. Sara didn't want a substitute parent. She needed a trusted friend and a mentor who believed in her.

Sara also helped Lynn and me formulate our parenting style. She taught us to raise our children to become mature adults by looking down the path to outcomes that helped us adjust short-term choices.

Sara came to our home to prepare for adult life and got more than she bargained for—a relationship with God and a second family. And we gained more than the joy of mentoring a teen. We watched God embrace a girl who poured out her heart in prayer through a window in her bedroom.

By His grace, we both received unexpected gifts.

Are You Serious, God?

By Angela J. Kaufman

Has God ever asked you to do something unusual?

My husband, Ron, and I try to be spiritually aware. In fact, Ron will often hear God tell him to do certain things. At the end of our day, we sometimes ask each other, "What is the latest thing God has asked you to do?" This is our way of checking in on each other's faith journey. We find that by doing this, we are more attuned to God, more aware of other's needs, and more open to being a vessel for God's work.

Ron is a psychologist and clinical director of an addiction treatment center. He knows that God's mission in his life is to help others hear His voice, so Ron spends time sitting in the quiet, waiting and listening. Communications will occur through words or images in Ron's mind, or from Scripture and the world around him. Ron shares stories with me of the nudges he receives from God. The topics may be odd, but the recipients feel affirmed at the right moment in their lives.

One time when Ron heard God's prompting, it seemed rather strange because it had nothing to do with helping anyone. In March 2000, a time of year when South Dakotans are weary of the long winter and filled with unrest, God told Ron to buy a $7,000 projector. Ron was so taken aback with this request that he resisted sharing the message with me. First, he reasoned, $7,000 is a lot of money! Even more than that, he could not imagine what need he would have for a projector, except to use at various events where he would speak. Surely God was not serious about owning a high-end projector, because conferences provide their own equipment for presenters.

Here I am! I stand at the door and knock. If anyone hears my voice and opens the door, I will come in.

—REVELATION 3:20 (NIV)

Ron decided not to buy the projector. Any reasonable person would conclude God's request was over. Right?

For the next few months, Ron did not feel as close to God as he had in the past.

He couldn't put his finger on what was wrong. Finally, early one morning in April, while listening to a preacher, he heard her say, "If you feel that something isn't right between you and God, go back and do the last thing God asked you to do." Well, the light bulb went on. Ron told me about the whole scenario, and we ordered the projector that same day.

The image projector arrived in a few weeks, and we eagerly unpacked it. We wanted to learn how it worked, so we gave it a test run. Then we put the device back in its case—and there it sat. April turned into May. One week, two weeks, three weeks. Spring turned into early summer.

On a sunny afternoon on June 8, 2000, police officers arrived at my husband's workplace. One of his coworkers had a daughter, Kellie, who had just been in a horrific car accident. We had many connections with her family through our youngest son's school, Ron's work, and our church.

Quickly, the sad truth spread throughout the community. Kellie and her lifelong best friend, Ashley, had been killed in a head-on collision with a truck. Alcohol was not involved, and it was unknown why their car crossed the center line on a road as flat and wide open as the prairies.

These two friends and vibrant Christians had grown up together, attended the same church, just completed their first year of college, and were well-known in our small town. A double funeral was planned at the local high school.

As preparations began for the service, Ron and I were involved because we are part of the worship team at church. The families wanted our group to provide music and help organize a PowerPoint that would share photographic memories of their lives. Ashley's grieving father, a teacher at the high school, knew the school would have the media technology we would need.

It was getting closer to the day of the funeral when we got word that the projector at the high school wasn't available. It had been sent away to be repaired as soon as school let out. Questions started flying. "Where will we find a projector on such short notice?" "Do you think businesses rent this type of equipment?"

Now, who do you suppose had a projector? A very expensive, high-powered projector, conducive for viewing in a large, bright auditorium on a summer's day? God's reason for telling Ron to purchase this item wasn't just a little obvious

> **Seek his will in all you do, and he will show you which path to take.**
>
> —PROVERBS 3:6 (NLT)

GOD'S GIFT OF TASTE

— By Eryn Lynum —

IN HONEY'S SWEET and nostalgic taste, one can perceive an incredible contribution of purpose. Each spoonful is an offering of noteworthy focus and determination. Bees never wander aimlessly. They don't slack off or procrastinate. Instead, their activity is a collaborative effort. Enjoying honey spread over warm bread or swirled into a steaming cup of tea, one experiences the intentionality God has threaded throughout creation. Philippians 2:13 (NIV) offers a taste of similar initiative God tucks into His children's hearts, "for it is God who works in you to will and to act in order to fulfill his good purpose."

---

to us. It was *overwhelmingly* obvious. Our feelings of joy and peace from being obedient to God's leading made us look at each other in speechless wonder.

God has a purpose in all that we are called to do. God is in the details of plans we know nothing about. God was working in advance to help the heartbroken families share God's love through their daughters' lives to an entire community. The prayer for a projector to be available was answered before anyone even knew to ask.

What is God asking you to do today?

Miracle Mission

By Lita Kharmai as told to Wanda Sanchez

I stepped off the plane and felt the blistering tarmac through the soles of my traveling shoes. The sweltering heat smothered me, but the sounds and smells brought a smile to my face—and memories of my childhood in Guyana, South America. I'd never imagined I'd return one day on a miracle mission.

A voice in the crowd caught my attention. "Jesus loves you. He died for your sins. Ask Him to take control of your life, and you'll live forever with Him in heaven!"

I eyed the curious man who had excitedly spoken these words. He spoke again. "Jesus loves you. Only He can give you hope and a future."

I'm not sure why, but I nodded—probably because I believed in Jesus, along with 33 million Hindu gods.

My parents practiced Hinduism, but I was nine years old when I first heard about Jesus at a street crusade. I also went to Sunday school and learned that Jesus died on a cross to save the world from our sins and give us eternal life. I was too busy for church, though.

I grew up poor and worked hard selling fruit on a street corner after school and homemade soap door-to-door on weekends. Every Saturday we rode a donkey cart to the market with my mother to sell groceries. Rain or shine, typhoon or heat wave, we were there. I knew then that I wanted to be a wife and mother—like my mother—and raise a family.

I looked at my daughter Nadira, standing beside me on the airport tarmac, and squeezed her hand. We were beginning God's adventure together.

> But Jesus said, "Let the little children come to me and do not hinder them, for to such belongs the kingdom of heaven."
>
> —MATTHEW 19:14 (ESV)

Growing up in Guyana, I'd felt compassion for disabled children. I knew a teenage boy who could not walk, talk, or move his arms, and it troubled me that his parents sat him in the market to beg. He couldn't communicate and was left alone every day in the hot sun. I didn't know then that God was preparing my heart to minister to the vulnerable.

In 1976 I moved to New York City, married my high school sweetheart, and started a family. Still confused, I searched for something but didn't know what. I longed to go to church but didn't know where. I'd been taught to worship all the Hindu gods and had idols in my apartment alongside a picture of Jesus, who I *wanted* to know.

In 1979 we moved from New York to Grand Rapids, Michigan, and a Baptist church faced our apartment. At the first opportunity, I grabbed our two-year-old son and headed to church, where I was warmly welcomed. There I learned about the one true God, Jesus Christ. That first Sunday I accepted Him as my God and immediately went home and tossed out every idol. My new life began that day.

But not my husband, Mancumar. Although he attended church with me, he did not share my faith.

Then in the spring of 2001, I received a surprising call. A missionary on the other end told me a compelling story. "I know a young girl who goes to church and loves it. But she can't walk. I believe her condition is called clubfoot."

"*Someone* must be able to help her," I muttered as I hung up the phone.

At that very moment God planted a seed in my heart that would birth a powerful ministry.

Shortly after, I was driving my daughter to an appointment, and a voice clearly said, "Lita, what are *you* going to do to help this little girl?"

I whipped my head around to see who'd whispered in my ear and saw my daughter's head bobbing to music from the radio. I contemplated the question until I knew what I had to do.

As our family grew to three children, God increased my compassion—and vision—for disabled children. One evening I shared my vision with my husband.

"God's given me an idea. He wants me to pray for and partner with doctors, host families, and hospitals in the US that can provide free medical care to children with disabilities from third world countries. I don't know why God thinks *I* can do this, but He's given me the vision, and I'm going for it!" My husband responded with total support.

I started a 501(c)(3) nonprofit called Children's Circle Mission, an organization to connect people around the world to offer hope to the medically hopeless.

Quickly, details came together. I talked with parents who had a daughter without an arm. I requested contact information for their daughter's surgeon, then reached out and asked for help pro bono. Although his office said no, they gave me the phone number for another surgeon's office. As I waited for word whether this doctor would help, I contacted an organization that agreed to help bring Preeya to the US.

Weeks later I was notified that a doctor was willing to perform surgery at no cost. My final prayers for an American host family and hospital services were also answered. God is faithful!

Encouraged, I decided to go to Guyana to interview other children who needed complex medical treatment. I'd prepared for my husband's shock when I told him.

"You're going to leave me…your children…your home… and go to Guyana for a stranger's child? We don't have money to pay for that! Besides, you have a full-time job with no paid time off. And you can't go without me."

I put down my teacup, smiled across the kitchen table, and said softly, "We have the money. And I want to take Nadira, so she can see where we come from. A trip to Guyana to see our birthplace and learn about our culture would be a wonderful educational opportunity for her."

My husband nodded. The creases at the corners of his eyes told me he was pleased.

Arrangements were quickly made for the trip to Guyana with our daughter. I took two weeks of unpaid leave from my job, planned details for family in my absence, and Nadira, my husband, and I were on our way.

A few days before we were to fly to Guyana to bring Preeya to the States for surgery, I fractured my rib. As painful as that injury is, nothing can be done to treat it.

"Can you postpone the trip for a couple of weeks?" I asked the trip director hopefully, holding my breath as I waited for her answer on the other end of the call.

"I'm sorry, Lita. This is the *only* opportunity."

Her words stirred an image of Jesus suffering on the cross. We met her at the airport the next day and collected our tickets.

When we landed in Guyana, we immediately met Preeya, an eleven-year-old girl with a big smile.

"She doesn't attend school because the children laugh at the way she walks and are cruel," her grandmother told us. "We're happy that Preeya will be able to walk like other children someday." Her eyes glistened.

Over the next few days, I gathered passport pictures and other needed documents and went to the US Embassy for Preeya's medical visa. I also showed our daughter Nadira the country, food, and customs of her heritage and shared childhood stories with her. My husband was so overwhelmed by the poverty he observed, he gave his life to Christ.

We came back to the US with Preeya, where she stayed with a Christian family and was homeschooled. After her surgery, her feet were normal. Preeya is a happy teenage girl and the people in her life are amazed at her transformation!

Since then, I've helped many children from different continents receive corrective surgery in the US. Every child and parent always hear about the extravagant love of Jesus Christ—the one true God—and how He called a simple woman to be His healing hands for His beloved children.

> **If anyone has material possessions and sees a brother or sister in need but has no pity on them, how can the love of God be in that person?**
>
> —1 JOHN 3:17 (NIV)

"You Matter!"

By Mindy Baker

During a time of great personal defeat in my life, my husband wanted me to travel overseas to help with his ministry organization, but I felt like I had nothing to contribute. His desire for me to participate more fully in his ministry coupled with my reluctance to do so were causing a huge chasm between us. He also wanted to take our three kids, who were sixteen, eighteen, and twenty at the time. No, no, no! I couldn't say it enough.

The events of the past five years had taken their toll. An ugly church split, the betrayal of close friendships, and a recent transition into a new job for my husband had left me feeling alone and set aside by God. I saw very clearly the miraculous way God had led my husband to this new good and purposeful work, but I did not see how I fit in. I felt set aside by God, as if I were the last person He would want to use for anything.

And then there was fear—the kind of illogical fear sent by the Enemy to grab you by your heart and twist it into an awful, anxious reality. The kind in which you cannot eat or sleep, but instead think of the worst-case scenario for every tiny detail of possibility for a particular situation. Fear that takes your breath away.

That was where I was living. I was a wounded, insecure woman plagued by fear and anxiety sent by demons of defeat, believing that God had set her aside and had no use for her. Yet God truly can and did make all things beautiful in His time.

My husband planned the trip, including me and all the kids. I said I would go. Half-heartedly, to be honest, but I wanted to move forward in my marriage and save face with our friends. What would they think if I refused to participate in this trip that was so important to my husband?

In the weeks that led up to the trip, I wasn't easy to be around. Through all the preparations and packing, I was terrified. I battled the fear with prayer, with praise, and with rehearsing the biblical truths about my Savior that my fears attempted to scorn. It was an intense battle.

You did not choose me, but I chose you and appointed you so that you might go and bear fruit—fruit that will last.

—JOHN 15:16 (NIV)

A day before our flight, something surprising took my breath away. I received a Facebook message from a missionary friend in Ecuador. Even though my friend Susan had been unaware of my trip, she stated that God had prompted her to message me.

As I read it, tears streamed down my cheeks.

"Father, remind Your precious daughter Mindy that You're holding her by the shoulders, looking into her eyes as You tell her: 'You are irreplaceable in My story. Your words matter. Your life matters. YOU matter. Will You trust Me today?' In Jesus's name. Amen."

I read the message over and over. Susan had no way of knowing the fear that had been gripping my heart, nor could she have known the sense of abandonment I was feeling from the Savior. She lived thousands of miles away and I had not disclosed the intensity of my emotional battle to anyone.

But God does not forsake us. And God had not forsaken me.

While in India, the plan was for me to hold women's conferences, something that is very rarely done in that culture. I was to be a table host, helping with discussions through the use of a translator. However, after the first session, the plans changed. The women wanted women speakers. The next thing I knew, a woman named Donna and I were to be the main speakers for the remaining sessions.

> **Never will I leave you; never will I forsake you.**
>
> —HEBREWS 13:5 (NIV)

Can you imagine what I used as the topics for my presentations? You guessed it! All of the things that God had taught me up until the moment I left on the trip. I talked about facing fears and battling our unseen enemies, how God never forsakes us, and how each of us matters and has a high calling to reach others for Christ. And with each group of women that we met, with tears in my eyes, I always concluded reading the Facebook message that I had received from Susan the night before the trip.

"You are irreplaceable in My story. Your words matter. Your life matters. YOU matter. Will you trust Me today?"

Each time I shared my story, it was always met with an emotional response from the audience. Many women testified that they felt the Holy Spirit stir their hearts as I spoke. That they could relate to the spiritual battles and the feelings of worthlessness. I realized that God prompted Susan to send this

GOD'S GIFT OF SIGHT
— By Lawrence W. Wilson —

A SCHOOL SOCIAL worker took boys from the inner city on adventure camping trips as a form of therapy. For most, it was their first experience outside the brightly lit urban center. The boys marveled at the number and density of the stars. "Where did they come from?" one boy asked. "They're always there," the guide said. "You just can't see them because the streetlights drown them out." The eye sees by taking in reflected light. Bright light, however, can make sight difficult. Sometimes it's necessary to remove the distraction of bright things to see what's really there.

---

message not only to encourage me in the moment of my struggle, but also to provide encouragement to many others whom I didn't even know I would meet or speak to.

I matter to God. He sees me. He loves me. He meets me at the point of my need when I call out to Him. Even when I couldn't see Him, His presence surrounded me. I take heart in knowing that God has good work for me to do for His glory.

When you make loving
others the story of your
life, there's never a final
chapter, because the legacy
continues. You lend your
light to one person, and he
or she shines it on another
and another and another.

—Oprah Winfrey

CHAPTER 3

Relationships Nurtured in Faith

A Case of
Mistaken Identity

By Mark Collins

At some young age—five? six?—I asked my father what his
job was.

"I'm a civil engineer," he said—but I only heard the "engineer" part. I imagined my dad at the helm of a large locomotive
chugging down the line, smoke billowing from the stacks, the
fireman loading another shovelful of coal from the tender.

"No, not that kind of engineer," my father said. "I design
things—buildings, transmission towers, things like that."

I'm sure I nodded, as if I understood; I did not. It would be
years before I fully appreciated what my father did for a living.

He was gifted with numbers, but unfortunately my father's
math genes were somehow lost in the wash before they got to
me. I tried my best, but algebra and its tricky cousin geometry
spelled the end to my technical career.

So, after trying several academic pursuits, I ended up with
an English degree, which always struck me as strange—to hold
a bachelor of arts in my native language. It's like training a dog
to bark: It doesn't take a whole lot of extra schooling, right?
It gets worse. After a few years I went back for a masters in
fine arts—in English. That's right: two advanced degrees in my
mother tongue.

What I didn't have was gainful employment. I had written a couple of short stories for a local literary magazine, but not much else. I used my MFA to deliver pizzas and deliver mail, though not at the same time.

Then, out of the blue, I got a call from the public relations department at my alma mater, the University of Pittsburgh.

"Is this Mark?" she asked.

"Yes," I said.

"Great! I'm an editor here at Pitt. We've been trying to reach you. I read your poem in the literary magazine and was really impressed. We were hoping you could write a feature for our recruitment brochure."

I was going to correct her—I had written a story, not a poem—but I didn't want to ruin her train of thought, which seemed to be a train carrying the possibility of money.

"Sure," I said.

"So what's your going rate for writing a freelance piece?" she asked.

I didn't have a rate, going or coming. I decided to go big.

"Ten dollars an hour," I said.

She paused. "You'll starve," she said. "We pay fifteen an hour."

> **The word of the LORD came to me, saying, "Before I formed you in the womb I knew you, before you were born I set you apart; I appointed you as a prophet to the nations." "Alas, Sovereign LORD," I said, "I do not know how to speak; I am too young."**
>
> —JEREMIAH 1:4–6 (NIV)

"Well," I said, "you drive a hard bargain, but OK."

I met with the editor the following day.

"Hello," I said. "I'm Mark Collins."

She peered at me over her half-rim glasses. "Collins? I thought your name was Smith."

"Not that I know of," I said.

She looked confused, but we started talking about the writing job, and we seemed to hit it off. Apparently I did OK with the freelance piece, because they hired me to do more.

Time passed. I kept writing. Eventually the editor confessed: She had originally intended to hire Mark *Smith*, the guy who wrote the poem. I got the gig by mistake, but it was too late to turn back.

My freelance job eventually led to a part-time position at *Pitt Magazine,* a job that included health benefits. This is no small item because our three small items—Faith, Hope, and Grace—were all born by C-section. Without insurance, the hospital bills would have exceeded my annual salary.

I began to collect some of my pieces into a manuscript, which—after a mere four dozen rejections—became a book, which happened to get the attention of an editor at *Daily Guideposts*, who contacted me about writing for them, which I have now been doing for the last twenty-five years. I even added three more books along the way.

It's not lost on me that the genesis of my professional life was predicated on a mistaken identity. Then again, most of my career has been about mistakes. That's what writing is. Write a draft, make many mistakes, then pick through the garbage of your prose, stripping off the stupid, culling the cliches. It is messy, undisciplined madness. Thanks to some smart, under-appreciated editor, my molten mass of writing sins will be gently exorcised and carefully reshaped into something readable and presentable to the world. (Trust me: It's better to enjoy the sausage than to watch how it's made.)

I can only imagine what my father would've made of this constant chaos. He'd probably faint if he saw the haphazard way I work. (Actually, even a train engineer would be shocked by the confusing disarray of my writing process, which lacks both neat tracks and any adherence to schedules.) By contrast, my dad's engineering work was a marvel of precision. He was part of the large team that designed the deep-dish space antennas that monitored the Apollo missions. Remember, this was the early 1960s, so many of the

> **For now we see only a reflection as in a mirror; then we shall see face to face. Now I know in part; then I shall know fully, even as I am fully known.**
>
> —1 CORINTHIANS 13:12 (NIV)

calculations were done with slide rules, not computers. I cannot fathom how he did this. Had I been a member of the design team…well, we'd still be waiting for one small step for man, one giant leap for mankind.

But I have no complaints. My life has been blessed, although it is far from orderly and certainly not mistake-free. I'll admit to some dark times when money was mighty tight, where my only currency was my faith—and even that was challenged. (Doubt, too, is part of the creative process—and not the fun part.) Yet I could not shake the feeling that Someone was there, even in the darkness.

GOD'S GIFT OF SIGHT
— By Lawrence W. Wilson —

FACIAL RECOGNITION SOFTWARE measures 80 points on a human face to calculate such things as the length of the nose, the depth of the eye sockets, and the shape of the cheekbones. Comparing the results to stored images, the software can correctly identify a person about 70 percent of the time. Human beings, by contrast, can store up to 10,000 faces in memory and recognize them in as little as 150 milliseconds, including identifying race, gender, mood, and approximate age. Despite advances in technology, the human brain remains the most reliable facial recognition system available.

Still, I ponder how my career would have turned out differently if the editor had called the right Mark instead of me.

Or maybe I *was* the right Mark, and neither of us knew it. Who can say? Maybe it was divine intervention—well, for me at least. Not so much for Mark Smith.

PS: Mr. Smith, if you're reading this—sorry about that.

The Amazing Eight

By Dana Waller as told to Wanda Sanchez

I met Nancy my first week of Bible college in September of 1979. We were both sitting in the chapel basement waiting to audition for a musical group. She struck up a conversation with me, and I'm pretty sure right then and there she decided we were kindred spirits and going to be lifelong friends.

Nancy was right, but I had no idea all those years ago that God Himself had sent her to me, and that her friendship, as well as others over time, would serve as a lifeline for me through some of the darkest days of my life.

Nancy and I spent the next thirty-nine years doing life together, raising our kids, visiting each other on holidays, and even taking vacations together. God gave me a tremendous blessing in Nancy's friendship, and I never took it for granted.

Some days in our lives become etched in memory. On March 9, 2018, I was sitting in a spartan medical office listening to a surgeon talk. I'd accompanied my husband, Mitch, to his post-op appointment, and I was holding his hand. He had recently undergone surgery to remove a brain tumor, and we were at the appointment to receive biopsy results. Although I was apprehensive, I had no idea what was coming as the surgeon looked at us solemnly.

The diagnosis was GBM—glioblastoma multiforme, the deadliest and most aggressive form of brain cancer possible.

I'd known the diagnosis was going to be bad and tried to prepare, but I hadn't realized how bad it could be. I heard the surgeon's voice droning on through my haze of shock. I did catch "...fifteen- to- twenty-four-month typical survival rate *with* treatment." As he continued talking, the world around me slipped into slow motion, yet my mind still could not grasp the words I was hearing. It was all surreal; feelings of immense sadness imprinted on my mind.

> **Perfume and incense bring joy to the heart, and the pleasantness of a friend springs from their heartfelt advice.**
>
> —PROVERBS 27:9 (NIV)

The following days and weeks moved forward in a blur of activity. Doctors' appointments, chemo, radiation, blood work, infusions, and more doctors' appointments. My mind and emotions remained numb to protect me.

Cancer respects no boundaries. It plays no favorites. It's indiscriminate. It can afflict the young or the old, the strong or the weak. It can blindside you in a heartbeat and turn your life upside down. It can suck every ounce of energy and shred every hope—*if* you let it.

Before I left the doctor's office that day, I knew that in the months and years to come, I was going to have to cling to God like never before.

I knew I'd need strength from Him I didn't possess. Strength to stand alongside my husband in the darkest days of his life—and mine. Strength I'd heard about and read about in Bible stories.

But a terminal diagnosis was our reality. Little did I know that, just like in every Bible story I'd heard about God's children facing a painful ordeal, God would indeed be there every moment and send me help and strength through my dear friend Nancy and seven other remarkable friends. The Amazing Eight, my gifts from God.

When Mitch and I got home the day of his diagnosis, I immediately called Nancy. As I unloaded my grief that day, she let me cry and cried *with* me like a true friend. I could feel God's love and strength in her words that day, as I did again and again over the next three and a half years.

After talking with Nancy, I called Kim, another close friend and member of the Amazing Eight. She, too, cried, prayed with me, and demonstrated what true friendship looks like. Kim and Nancy sent out word to our whole group, and they rallied around Mitch and I in a concerted demonstration of love, support, and compassion that still makes me weep with overwhelming gratitude. It is difficult to describe the restorative role of love and care when we are suffering beyond our limits so we can find our hope in Jesus.

You see, I belong to an incredible, rare sisterhood. Years ago, we were young mothers in desperate need of a break from children's chatter, teen drama, and endless to-do lists. We needed adult conversations and laughter with our own kind. We needed affirmation, prayer, hugs, and camaraderie. By God's design, we found one another, and every summer we scheduled our "Wives Weekend Away" to recharge. The nine of us. Each year we found a cabin in the mountains or a house at the beach to relax, talk, laugh, share life, and most importantly, pray. Each year we'd keep track of everyone's prayer requests and talk about what God had done in our lives.

Those years of friendship and fellowship formed an extraordinary bond between us.

We all have adult children and grandchildren now. We've shared life's challenges—childbirth, marriage, divorce, job loss, sickness, cancer, and death. We've also shared life's joys, as well as stories so funny we laugh until we cry, not to mention our "besties shenanigans." But the bond that is the strongest between us is our faith in God. Every additional year we have together, I marvel at the connection God forged among us. The spiritual strength we have drawn from one another has shaped the course of our lives.

> **Above all, love each other deeply, because love covers over a multitude of sins. Each of you should use whatever gift you have received to serve others, as faithful stewards of God's grace.**
>
> —1 PETER 4:8, 10 (NIV)

When Mitch was diagnosed with brain cancer, the Amazing Eight rallied around me. Hilary sat for hours with me in the hospital waiting room. Kim dropped what she was doing to fly up from California to help me. Nancy and her family spent a week helping us on our farm. Lori, Denise, Pam, Fran, and Jeannette prayed for Mitch and me every single day. They sent our prayer request around the world. They believed with us for a miracle. They sent cards, gifts, and provided meals. They video chatted with us or me at least three or four times a week. On days that I wanted to get out and drive, because home was too painful a place to be, they talked me through my sorrow. Every day of my grief, they walked with me through the fire and lifted me up. They were the hands of God guiding, protecting, encouraging, supporting. Without them I probably would have collapsed under the weight of hardship and grief.

My precious Mitch left us in June 2021. He is in heaven now, wrapped in the arms of Jesus. Through the difficulties of his homegoing and the weight of responsibility that fell on me, my selfless friends stood beside me again, helping with every detail, loving and praying me through it all.

Riches can't always be deposited in a bank. I am *rich* beyond compare with God's riches and one of His most valuable blessings of true friendship. I can see His face in the faces of my precious, extraordinary "sisters," who showed me how ordinary people can do extraordinary work for God.

You Lyft Me Up

By Wanda Sanchez

"See you in another couple of months!" I shouted back into the church at the pastor, my friend Dawn, as I stepped outside to wait for my ride.

It was a beautiful, bright, and chilly fall day in Rockford, Michigan. Too bright for my sensitive eyes, so I closed them and tipped my head up to catch the warmth of the sun on my face.

I sighed inwardly as familiar uneasiness washed over me. My concern was a fact of life related to my legal blindness (combined with unmarried status) and dependency upon others to get me where I needed to go. But in the past weeks, it had seemed really hard to get a driver to show up for my transport in the small, beautiful town that I call home. I had an almost daily need for someone to drive me to important medical appointments, client appointments, church, the bank, grocery store, and other places as needed. I often paid for these services in advance, only to be left standing on my porch reading a cancellation notice among my text messages.

It wore on my soul to be dependent on people and businesses that weren't reliable and couldn't seem to help me accomplish my personal business and tasks. It is impossible for me to describe the enormous turmoil that had stalked my life because of being dependent on undependable means of transportation. Sometimes I ordered rides and they were not available. Other times, they were scheduled, but they did not show up. Yet other times they arrived too late to get me where I needed to go. Often, the transportation company I was calling did not answer their phone. And on other occasions, I would be scheduled for an appointment or asked to participate in an event the day before or the day of, and my needs required me to schedule a ride a week in advance.

> **And let us consider how we may spur one another on toward love and good deeds... encouraging one another.**
>
> **—HEBREWS 10:24–25 (NIV)**

I opened my eyes and disinterestedly scanned the parking lot for a possible ride. (I still have limited vision, which is degenerating.) My frustration and resignation were mounting as a sleek black SUV pulled into the driveway directly in front of me.

An enthusiastic voice called out, "Wanda?"

"Yep! Dana?" I asked, calling out the name of the driver I'd been assigned.

"That's me. Hop in!" she answered as she scurried to help me with the door. I got in the back seat and away we went to conquer big things. Well, not really. I was only headed to my apartment, but I was grateful for a clean car and a punctual and perky driver.

"Thanks for accepting my ride. I don't know if it's Covid or something else, but it's sure been a challenge getting rides lately. I really appreciate it!"

And I meant it. I felt like I could take a deep breath and relax. Before we were out of the parking lot, Dana and I had become friends. Our chatter was comfortable and easy, and I knew in my heart that we would eventually do things together.

Our ride was short, but we managed to cover a lot of territory in that first conversation. She was a few years younger than me, a wife and mother of two young children. She made friends everywhere she went, but sometimes preferred puppies to people. As we talked rapid-fire and poured out information about ourselves, we often found ourselves exclaiming, "Me too!" as we found shared interests and common ground.

Too soon we pulled into the driveway of the small ranch house where I lived. She turned around in the seat, and I saw a dark-haired beauty. I'd already figured out she was brave and smart.

"Thank you so much, Dana! You're the coolest driver I've ever had, and you made this ride so much fun."

She lifted her sunglasses onto her head and looked me in the eye. "When you need to get somewhere, Wanda, let me know a day ahead, and I'll take your ride. I drive five days a week, and it's not a problem."

I struggled for words. I didn't know how to respond. She couldn't possibly know what it would mean to me to have a driver I could depend on. A driver who would really show up and not leave me standing and waiting. This would relieve one of the greatest pressures in my life—one that I'd been praying about for months, maybe a year. In this moment with Dana, I knew once again that God was showing me that He had my back. This was something only He could have managed. I would never have thought I'd have a professional driver in my phone contacts.

"Really? I don't know what to say. It would be a *huge* relief for me to be able to depend on a ride when I needed one. You have no idea..." I glanced down as I felt my eyes getting moist. I would not cry, but I was overwhelmed.

I could feel her looking at me. She repeated her offer. "You'd better let me know, OK?" she said with a fake threat in her voice.

"I'd love that. Thank you so much."

That was the first and last day I sat in the back seat of Dana's car and the last day she *ever* accepted money for a ride from me. After that first time, she wouldn't let me pay, no matter how hard I tried. I ended up hiding money in her car, then texting a message about where to find it after she dropped me off at home.

We laughed and talked about our lives when she drove me wherever I needed to go. She talked about her work and family, and I talked about my family and work as a writer and speaker as a PTSD/trauma consultant. We whispered girl secrets into each other's curious ears. We talked about faith...and I apologized to her more than once for not being a "good" Christian when she saw me lose my temper or display an inappropriate attitude. We talked about deep things of faith as I told her about my life trauma, and she opened up and told me about hers.

One day we sat in the car sipping large, hot mochas, listening to the rain on the car roof. Dana turned to me and said, "You're always saying thank you and telling me how grateful you are to me. I appreciate that, but, Wanda, I've learned so much from you. I never cry, but I'm about to right now because the things I've learned from you have helped me so much! I'm the one who's grateful!"

During one of the most difficult and dark times in my life, the good God I serve sent Dana into my life to offer her unique support and to fill a desperate need. She also furnished a rental home I'd moved into with her own beautiful belongings. She purchased items for the house and never asked for anything in return. It never seemed to occur to her to ask for anything but my friendship. I happily offered my hand of sisterhood in return.

> **Do nothing out of selfish ambition or vain conceit. Rather, in humility, value others above yourselves, not looking to your own interests but each of you to the interests of the others.**
>
> —PHILIPPIANS 2:3–4 (NIV)

The symbiotic nature of our relationship taught both of us many things. I'm grateful for the investment Dana made in my life and equally as grateful for the time I've been able to invest in her life and help her too. I'm honored that she shared her story with me and has allowed me to speak into her life. I've seen her begin to process things in her life where she's been "stuck."

Watching the whole concept of reciprocity come alive in this friendship has ushered in an awareness and beautiful example of community and how it's supposed to work. God brought Dana came into my life when I was grieving deep losses. My vision had seriously deteriorated, and my best friend had moved far away from me. I felt lost and was having difficulties adjusting to the changes. My needs could have scared off someone less brave, but Dana was God's gift—an advocate who helped lift and tend my soul in a season when I was unable to advocate for myself.

My Last Game

By Dr. Jay Morris

I sat by the curb under the streetlight shadow, slumped against a lamppost and barely visible from the road. Behind me, William Allen Stadium was still and dark. The annual inner-city Thanksgiving Day football game between William Allen High School and Louis E. Dieruff High School was finally over. Dieruff had won. The lights from the stadium and clubhouse were out, 15,000 fans were long gone, and I sat alone, waiting for Dad to pick me up as I pondered the devastating realization that I would never play football again.

Two knee surgeries had relegated me to the second team as a senior tailback, but only in the darkness after the game had I finally grasped the reality that my football career was over.

I began trembling and weeping uncontrollably. I felt as if I'd lost my life. My dreams were gone. What was I going to do? Football had *always* been my identity and my future, and futures and identities came hard in my family.

When my grandfather was sober, he was my babysitter and best friend. He taught me to pray and was the only family member who encouraged and convinced me to go to college. My parents were hardworking and loving but struggled to keep our household together, and at the age of four, I was pretty much on my own.

Eventually, Dad arrived in our 1970 green Pinto and I climbed in. He was never late and was always silent—it was just his way.

Life in Lehigh Valley, Pennsylvania, centered around football. About thirty-five men from the Valley played in the NFL, including Chuck Bednarik and Andre Reed, two NFL Hall of Famers. I started playing at the Allentown Union Street Boys Club at age nine. But my journey to Division 1 college football came to a jolting halt when I walked off the field for the last time—November 26, 1970.

As a sophomore, I attended Louis E. Dieruff High School with friends I'd known since grade school. At the end of that year, Mom and Dad moved our family to a different part of Allentown. The move took me away from my friends and put me in a school with only five other students of color.

> **But he disciplines us for our good, that we may share his holiness. For the moment all discipline seems painful rather than pleasant, but later it yields the peaceful fruit of righteousness to those who have been trained by it.**
>
> —HEBREWS 12:10–11 (ESV)

My career was over by the beginning of my junior season, but I stayed on the team and rode the bench, playing in only two games. I was scheduled to start in my third game when I suffered my second knee injury the night before the game. I was taken to the hospital by ambulance.

I had no doubts that I could still play, but I needed to hear others express their confidence in me. So far that year, I'd sat on the bench and had failed at the thing I loved most.

The years that followed were painful. Because I wasn't aware of His presence, I didn't realize the Holy Spirit was with me. I'd gone to church with my parents as a child, but I didn't understand that God allows His children to go through hardships so they can be refined by fire. Although the process can feel unbearable, we're often most open to the Spirit of God in these moments.

Following that game, the Holy Spirit protected *my* spirit by sheltering me from long-term anger and bitterness, which is dangerous, especially for God's children. Although I was in the furnace and felt abandoned, the Holy Spirit kept me from becoming hostile, combative, and jealous. He showed me how to develop patience and self-control. Weeping brought a release that purged my frustration and restored my soul with God's comfort.

When the season was over, I was totally lost. Then in January of 1971, as I was walking between classes, a teacher approached me in the hallway and said, "Make something out of your life."

"I'll try," I answered.

"No," he responded. "Either you do, or you don't." End of conversation.

His assurance about me sank deep into my being. I'd never been in his classes or talked to him before that day. I'd only seen him at a distance. His encouragement was balm to my soul.

I'd accepted Jesus when I was thirteen and was an excellent student, but by middle school, I'd abandoned interest in studying and learning, including about Jesus. All I cared about was sports and hanging out. Football was my first love. I randomly applied to three colleges in February of my senior year. I was accepted by North Carolina Central University in Durham, North Carolina, which was a miracle, given my abysmal grades and application submitted in February of my senior year. One school sent me a rejection letter, and the third never responded.

No one ever talked to me about college, except Pop, my paternal grandfather. I didn't know anyone to ask for advice about applying to or paying for college. My parents and grandparents did not possess the means. In passing, I told Nick Fragnito, the executive director of the local boys' club, that I was applying to college and desperately needed money.

"Nick, I don't know how to pay for college. I don't have any money. I always thought I'd get a football scholarship."

"Let me see what I can do," Nick replied. I never thought about our conversation again.

Then later that spring, Nick gave me a check for $500, which was a lot of money in 1971. Enough to get this kid to college.

It's been fifty-two years since I sat on that curb with a broken heart. I hadn't thought about that day, that game, or the lamppost for decades, but this morning when I woke up, God put that memory in my heart. Before noon I was asked to tell that story to you. Young Jay had no mentors to give him guidance, but if I could speak into his life on that day, I'd say this:

> "Jay, God loves you more than you can imagine. He has given you an Advocate—Jesus—to guide you, comfort you, fight for you, lead you in truth, and who will never leave you, no matter how dire your circumstances (John 14:15–17). Cling to that truth. Your heart is broken over football, and you feel lost. Release your heartache and circumstances to God, and let your tears cleanse your soul.

Yes, you are losing something dear, but God has another plan for your life—more than you would ask for or imagine.

"The Holy Spirit that sits on that curb with you today is the same Holy Spirit who sits with all of us in our losses. He has plans for all our lives."

I recently retired from a job I loved that I probably wouldn't have ever held if I hadn't hurt my knee and abandoned my dream of being a football player. Although I've made plenty of mistakes, God has forgiven me and blessed me with abilities, opportunities beyond my dreams, a wife beyond value, and a loving family. He has always enabled me to land on my feet, though sometimes a little off-balance. I've survived terrible situations in my life but experienced God's peace even though circumstances around me caused fear and doubt. I know God is the creator of all things, and I can trust Him unconditionally.

God had a different plan for my life than I had. His Word tells me He knew me before I was born and recorded every day and moment of my life in His book (Psalm 139:16). God has a plan in our suffering for all of us.

God's peace surpasses all understanding, which is what I experienced weeping at the lamppost. The Holy Spirit was with me then, He is with me now, and He is with you too.

Have hope! No matter what game you're in, it's not over!

A Tiny Room Filled with Hospitality

By Lynne Hartke

"Walk the plank."

Every pirate movie I had ever watched went through my mind as I stared at the rough board at my feet. The words didn't come from a cutlass-wielding buccaneer, however, but from Agus, our five-foot-tall Indonesian host and interpreter. He did not stand on the deck of a three-masted galleon but at the entrance to a small fishing village constructed on wooden stilts above the Java Sea. The only way into the village was on a wooden sidewalk, consisting of a series of planks—also on stilts—above the water.

What had I gotten myself into?

My husband, Kevin, and I had traveled to visit friends involved in a literacy program established in libraries on several of the 600 inhabited islands in Indonesia, an archipelago country stretching over 3,200 miles, from east to west, between the Indian and Pacific Oceans.

After visiting several city libraries, we were excited about touring a village library, home of the Bajau people, also known as sea gypsies. At one time a nomadic group, the ocean wanderers had spent most of their lives in the past on simple boats, only coming to shore to barter for what they could not make themselves or harvest from the sea. With the decrease of fishing populations, many now lived in simple villages built on wooden stilts, located a few miles from the mainland, with their beloved sea beneath them.

"Where's the library?" we asked a group of boys listening to a boom box at the entrance to the sea village. The boys pointed in the distance, to a destination I could not see. All I saw was the elevated wooden sidewalk I needed to cross.

"Walk the plank," Agus repeated, this time with a smile.

I stared at the series of rough planks, nailed together in a single rickety path that wobbled six feet above the water. Taking a deep breath, I took a tentative step on the first board. Did the board sway side to side or was it the waves beneath me?

Share with the Lord's people who are in need. Practice hospitality.

—ROMANS 12:13 (NIV)

Two young boys swam in their shorts, darting between the stilts. Known as excellent free divers, Bajau children learned to swim before they learned to walk. Eventually they would dive as much as sixty feet to the ocean floor while holding their breath for as long as five minutes. Using homemade spear guns, they would hunt for fish and octopi.

With no octopi in sight, the curious boys watched me inch across one board and then another. As seafoam churned in sync with the waves, I remembered having to take beginner swim lessons three times as a child because I didn't like putting my face in the water.

What happens when cell phones get wet? I wondered, as I stepped onto plank three. *What happens when library visitors get wet?*

"You can do it!" encouraged Kevin, already safe—and dry—on the other side.

Dear God, help me, I pleaded silently as I stepped onto the fourth board held in place with one rusty nail. I prayed the words to a promise I once learned in Sunday school: "When you pass through the waters, I will be with you; and through the rivers, they shall not overwhelm you" (Isaiah 43:2, ESV).

I stepped off board five and onto the final board. "Let there be no overwhelming water today, Jesus," I prayed as I adjusted my balance before I stepped onto the solid rock perimeter bordering the village. The gathered crowd kept me from doing a victory dance.

"This way," Agus said, motioning us to the village school that housed the library.

The door was closed. Locked.

"School testing this week," a woman explained, her words translated for our benefit. "Half day."

We nodded, accepting a common education reality around the world. Unsure what to do, we stood around in the blistering heat with 90 percent humidity. The circle of sweat on my cotton T-shirt widened exponentially with each ticking minute.

"Come into this home," Agus said, motioning us into a blue house with a corrugated metal roof. "Have a seat, have a seat."

The woman and homeowner directed me to a far corner. Candies and other snacks hung down from the ceiling. The home was also a store.

I gratefully accepted the owner's offerings of simple crackers and bottled water. As I watched her move around the room in her long, red sundress, I wondered if I would be so gracious as to welcome a group of foreigners wandering around my neighborhood in Arizona. If our roles were reversed, would I open my home to strangers? Would I offer my livelihood to refresh them?

"Can you share a story with the mothers and children who are here about the importance of reading?" Agus asked me once we were all served. Several women, along with dozens of children, now filled the tiny room.

I gulped. What could I possibly share that had any relevance to a sea gypsy whose home was smaller than my kitchen? What did I have in common with a woman who lived with open-air windows and walk-the-plank sidewalks?

Also, I wasn't the expert. I came to Indonesia as a simple observer to view the literacy program. I didn't come with facts and figures and the latest data of school dropout rates.

The homeowner passed out another round of crackers and water, offering what she had. In a culture of oral stories and traditions, could I do the same?

"Do you have a story?" Agus asked again.

I cleared my throat. I didn't have a story about a mother raising kids by the sea, but I knew a story of a woman raising children on a farm without much money or luxuries—my grandmother.

"My grandfather on my father's side had to drop out of school at a young age," I began, "after the death of his father. My grandmother had more education," I added, knowing the value of elders in the village. "My grandfather owned a dairy farm, and every night after the farmwork was done, my grandmother would read to the seven children."

Agus interpreted my words, while Kevin added a few barnyard sound effects as the children listened, entranced.

"My father was one of those seven children. He was the first in his family to go to the university," I continued. "He became a teacher."

The homeowner leaned forward, focusing on my words. Did she also yearn for a university education for her children?

"My father's success began, in part, with his mother reading to him," I concluded, thankful for the legacy of my heritage that bonded me to my listeners. My grandmother had not allowed what she lacked to prevent her from serving what she had to her family.

> **And you will be blessed. Although they cannot repay you, you will be repaid at the resurrection of the righteous.**
>
> **—LUKE 14:14 (NIV)**

Before we left, the homeowner motioned her children forward to sing a song about going to school and learning their lessons so they wouldn't get in trouble. They laughed and sang while their mom clapped along, serving us, her guests, with music and entertainment.

While they sang, excuses I had used in the past to keep me from having people into our home raced through my mind.

You can't come over. My house isn't clean.
I will have you over after I remodel the kitchen.
My schedule is too busy right now.

I pondered my excuses as I watched the sea through the slats in the floor, flowing back and forth. Back and forth. God had answered my prayer earlier, not allowing the water to

GOD'S GIFT OF HEARING
— By Eryn Lynum —

CONTRASTING THE SINGLE vocal cord of humans, God created songbirds with a dual set of vocal cords known as a syrinx. With this set of singing organs, birds are able to produce two sounds simultaneously. An individual bird offers an orchestral production from an overhanging branch, raising an anthem of praise to the Creator! In the bird's multilayered melody, one can perceive the many tones and notes of God's creation. Worship is not a one-size-fits-all experience but a creative and uniquely individual means of engaging with God.

---

overwhelm me as I walked the planks into the village. I realized I had allowed my excuses to overwhelm me, drowning my hospitality. God was here with me as I learned to flow with my circumstances, offering what I had, like my grandmother—and this woman—before me.

The homeowner smiled as the children began another song. She offered no apology or complaint as more children arrived on the front porch. They pressed against the metal screen covering the front window, joining the song, while the sea and the woman swayed.

My heart bent to the motion.

Back and forth. Back and forth.

Living in the Same Neighborhood All Along

By Michelle Van Loon

I was living in what I called my "lame duck" period of life when I met Jeanna. I was a wife and mother beginning to phase out of my place in my community in preparation for an out-of-state relocation, and Jeanna was the "new kid in town." At the time, I never imagined our connection would outlast most of the friendships I'd carefully cultivated during the years our family lived in Crystal Lake, Illinois.

A lame-duck period in politics is the time after an election and before a previously elected leader steps out of his or her role. My stepping-out period was much less public and more personal. I was a suburban homeschooling mom living out the awkward period between telling people we'd be relocating in the annoyingly distant future and the day the moving van finally showed up at our home.

My lame duck period, unfortunately, meant my friends often made plans for events and excluded my family and me. I could emotionally feel the gears of my relationships with other homeschool moms begin to downshift, and it was awkward and painful. I counted many of these women as close friends, but, sadly, my changing departing status revealed otherwise. Relationships I'd thought of at best friend level quickly devolved to casual friendships and occasional conversations. I knew that transitions in our lives can carry grief as one chapter ends and a new one is yet to begin. But that in-between zone can also make space in our lives for new gifts.

My budding friendship with Jeanna soon taught me that the only thing that might be more socially awkward than being a lame duck was being the new kid. Trying to figure out where you fit in as a newcomer is an enormous challenge, whether you're a first grader on an unfamiliar playground or an adult transplanted into a new community. Jeanna was searching for information about a home-school enrichment group I'd helped organize in our community, and she reached out to me shortly after she moved to town. I experienced a few moments of sadness when I realized I wouldn't be fielding inquiries like hers much longer. Soon, like her, *I'd* be looking for connections in a new town.

> **If you really keep the royal law found in Scripture, "Love your neighbor as yourself," you are doing right.**
>
> **—JAMES 2:8 (NIV)**

While my family was still living in Crystal Lake, I did what I could to help Jeanna feel welcome in the enrichment group. In the beginning of our relationship, our conversations centered on our kids and our shared activities in the group. Jeanna's warm, welcoming personality and her living faith in God made me feel like we'd known each other for years instead of weeks. Her desire to seek God in the disorienting experience of transplanting to a new community was a model for me as I would be facing the same thing soon.

Our oldest children enjoyed spending time together in the months before our move, which was an unexpected gift during the transition periods both of our families were experiencing. After our move to a city two hours north of Crystal Lake, the friendship between our kids continued. Every few months Jeanna and I drove to meet in a shopping center parking lot halfway between our homes on Friday afternoons. We dropped off or picked up each other's oldest children so they could spend weekends together at our homes. We'd meet up again on Sunday and send the visiting child back home. But our kid-swapping also kept us in touch and helped build our friendship. And our friendship ignited my faith as I was struggling to acclimate to my new community.

The apostle Paul wrote these words to his friends in Thessalonica to urge them to continue to provide spiritual and practical support to one another in a difficult and changing world: "Therefore encourage one another and build each other up, just as in fact you are doing" (1 Thessalonians 5:11, NIV). Even then, Jeanna stayed in the category of "mom coworker" for a time. But the nature of our relationship changed when Jeanna's mom, who lived in a distant city, was diagnosed at age fifty-one with colon cancer. Our friendship shifted from two homeschool moms sharing information about our kids' activities and organizing weekend visits into a relationship shaped by shared prayer. Sadly, her mom fought valiantly, but passed too young.

I didn't realize it at the time, but praying for Jeanna's mom enrolled me in a different kind of school of learning as I interceded for her family. This classroom didn't have anything to do with reading, writing, or arithmetic, but taught me, instead, how to journey through the valley of the shadow. Jeanna modeled for me how to celebrate the gift of her mom's life as she savored every moment with her mom during her illness. Jeanna continued to honor her life as she grieved the immeasurable loss of her mom's passing. She shared frequent anecdotes about her mom in our conversations, and those memories blessed me too.

I didn't understand how much Jeanna taught me until much later. She and I continued to stay in touch through life changes and relocations. Jeanna moved to northern Florida, and I ended up back in the Chicago area. No matter how long it had been since we'd spoken, we always managed to pick up right where we'd left off. While we updated each other on what our kids were doing, Jeanna always made it a priority to talk about the things that matter most in life: grace, forgiveness, and joy.

In 2007, my mom, who lived in south Florida, was diagnosed with terminal breast cancer and was placed in hospice care. I flew across the country to care for her in her final weeks of life. Because of the speed of her decline, I felt like I'd parachuted into uncharted territory. I was grateful for the many expressions of concern from friends back home, but among the most meaningful to me were check-in phone calls from Jeanna. I didn't have to explain my emotions, silence, or questions to her. She knew what I was going through, and I knew she was praying.

After my mom's funeral, I packed up her old car and prepared to make the long trip home. Jeanna called to find out how I was holding up.

"I know you're focused on getting home, but why not stop and join me for a cup of coffee," she urged. "I'll meet you at a coffee shop near the interstate." The location wasn't exactly in her backyard, but the moment she suggested we meet, I knew there was nothing I needed more than to see my old friend.

It wasn't until I saw Jeanna's face in that noisy restaurant that I realized how depleted I was. For weeks, I'd been caring round-the-clock for my mom's physical needs. My sister had arrived from out-of-state to give me respite, but my mom died within hours of her arrival. We worked to put together the funeral service, then emptied Mom's house in preparation for selling it. I'd been so busy completing urgent tasks that I hadn't had a chance to stop and *feel* my grief.

> **Carry each other's burdens, and in this way, you will fulfill the law of Christ.**
>
> —GALATIANS 6:2 (NIV)

I didn't have to explain any of this to Jeanna. Her hug that day told me she saw every unshed tear in my heart. I'd been privileged to break tiles and help lower her through the roof to Jesus for healing. Now it was my turn. (See Mark 2:1–12 and Luke 5:17–26.) Comfort poured from her without a word.

Poet Samuel Taylor Coleridge said, "Friendship is a sheltering tree." In that noisy restaurant that day, I was profoundly grateful for the sanctuary of the slow-growing, deeply rooted tree of friendship planted by God that sheltered me…and Jeanna. Though we'd only lived in the same zip code for a short time a long time ago, in all the most important ways, my friend Jeanna and I had lived in the same neighborhood all along.

Let Him Go

By Virginia Ruth

"I don't think I can continue."

Those words from our son were words we were not expecting to hear. My husband and I were in the kitchen preparing dinner when our son called, which he did whenever he had a chance. Recently the calls were becoming more frequent and lengthier. He was in his first year of medical school, which had begun in the midst of the COVID-19 lockdown. He was still isolated in his apartment. Most days he spent twelve to sixteen hours in front of the computer listening to his professors, with no interaction from anyone else.

As the sausage sizzled on the stove, we were struggling to hear our son speak. Quietly my husband, John, turned off the burner. "We better sit down," he mouthed to me.

We sat across from each other at the table with our phone on speaker. Henry vented all the trouble he was having. More than any logistics, he was questioning the motives and means of getting this degree. His view became more global and existential.

"What is the point?" he questioned. "I might start out with noble ideas for medicine but the reality is, it's all about the money. I'm going to put all this time into training, and for what? To spend only ten minutes with a patient because I have to keep moving them along?"

As Henry was speaking and I was intently listening, the voice inside my head was screaming, *What do you mean? You were the one who pursued this option in your life. You shadowed doctors and saw practices. You were the one who took extra schooling so that you could get into medical school—at quite an expense for us, I might add. You were the one who had a plan.*

Of course, I could not say those words out loud when Henry was so distraught. Instead, we offered gentle reassurances and suggestions to sleep on the decision and pray about it, and we suggested we talk in the morning.

As we hung up, I thought of all the times when, as parents, we had guided our children through life. Times when we had to make the decisions about their direction: what preschool to attend, which playmates for playdates, even what activities they would be engaged in. As they became adults, we had no choice in their decision for school, work, friends, and social opportunities. Most days we did not know what they were doing. Each morning we would offer perfunctory prayers for their well-being and were generally pleased with the "wise" decisions they were making.

> **Your words were found, and I ate them, and your words became to me a joy and the delight of my heart, for I am called by your name, O LORD, God of hosts.**
>
> —JEREMIAH 15:16 (ESV)

But now, the idea that Henry would quit school and not pursue his decision to become a doctor was beyond my acceptance.

I felt I could not just offer gentle guidance, but I knew I couldn't bully him into a decision. When he had been speaking, I could hear that he was not in optimal physical or mental health.

That night I tossed and turned. In my mind's eye I stood in front of the throne of God, pacing back and forth and asking Him to keep Henry safe and in a good frame of mind to make a decision.

Why are You testing him? Testing us? I demanded of God. *What happened?* I began telling God all about Henry: *He enjoyed science and medicine. He was a good student, intelligent and usually unflappable. He would make a wonderful doctor. He wanted to help people. What would he do instead?*

I fretted over Henry's physical and fragile mental health: *There is no break for years. He has to be able to function with very little sleep. Is he feeling so desperate he would take his life?*

And then I worried: *Once he makes a decision, that would be it. He would never be able to return.* Medical school was highly competitive. He would be throwing away that opportunity. My thoughts were getting darker and more worrisome.

"He was Mine before he was yours." I heard God say gently as I lay awake. Various verses kept running over and over in my head: "Do not be anxious about anything, but in every situation, by prayer and petition, with thanksgiving, present your requests to God" (Philippians 4:6, NIV). God reminded me that he made Henry and knew all about him: "For I know the plans I have for you…plans to prosper" (Jeremiah 29:11, NIV).

I spoke back to God. *I am going out on a faith limb and trusting You, Lord, that You have a plan for Henry's life.* I felt myself gradually relinquishing Henry over to God's care and presence.

God's message seemed particularly merciful. Over the years, when Henry would come home for a visit, we'd ask if he would go to church with us. He always found an excuse. When we would ask if he found a church where he was living, he would hem and haw and give us one of a number of excuses.

Finally, we inquired about his faith. "I do not believe in the existence of God," came his reply.

I was blown away. This was the child who seemed to enjoy going to church, who had volunteered with middle school fellowship while in high school, and had even contemplated becoming a youth pastor.

We had tried to guide Henry through the years. We took the admonition "train up a child" seriously, yet I wondered if we pushed our beliefs on him. Could we have modeled our faith better?

His final decision to drop out of medical school after a year threw me for a loop, but the renouncing of his faith set me in a low place. I was anxious and panicky about our son's future as well as ashamed and guilt-ridden for not being a better spiritual parent.

Once again, I found myself on my knees, fretting to God. This time I felt like Jacob wrestling with the stranger to be blessed. I wanted something from God—His assurance that Henry was His and that He would not let Henry go.

What is happening, Lord? Where have You been in my prayers for Henry's well-being? I had just gotten to a place of acceptance about medical school and now this. I thought You were with him. I thought You were with us.

Little did I know that my turning over Henry's vocational plans to God was just the beginning. Instead of Henry learning to trust God with his future, I was the one who had to trust God more and more with Henry's future. I had to take a leap of faith that God would handle this. In a way, I was acting as if

God did not exist: I had negated any prior lessons learned that God was a very near presence in my child's life and mine. I felt that God had abandoned me and my request as a mother.

I thought that God would be surrounding our family in ways we could feel. What I discovered through my evening tussles with God was that He is always present even when we cannot see Him. In my wrestling, God reminded me of all the times in my journey when I, too, had questioned His control and presence in my life. He reminded me that even at those times, He was there with me always and I had to learn to lean on Him. And now it was my son's turn.

> **Behold, I am with you and will keep you wherever you go, and will bring you back to this land. For I will not leave you until I have done what I promised you.**
>
> **—GENESIS 28:15 (ESV)**

"I have him," I heard God say to my heart. "You can let go of Henry and let Me, who created him, guide his journey whether Henry realizes it or not."

Just as I had to learn to let go of our son physically, I also realized that I had to let Henry go spiritually, knowing he is ultimately God's and not mine. God will not abandon our son. It is in my letting go that I realized God never has and never will let go of any of His children.

I thought faith would say "I'll take away the pain and discomfort." But what it ended up saying was "I'll sit with you in it." I never thought until I found it that that would be enough.

—Brené Brown, author

CHAPTER 4

The Healing Power of God

A Stranger's Steadying Prayer

By Eryn Lynum

"You are fine to fly out tomorrow."

I heard the doctor's words, but they were hollow. They landed in the shallow soil of my mind, refusing to root down. Despite his best intentions to help, I didn't trust his decision. More accurately, I doubted my ability to board a plane and fly home in the morning.

Overwhelming dizziness had landed me in the emergency room in an unfamiliar city. With no diagnosed cause, I was cleared to leave and return home to Colorado and my family.

The following day, I woke with nervous jitters in my stomach and the same swimming feeling in my head. Through the bag check-in line and security, I tried convincing myself I could do this. I have flown across the world numerous times. Surely I could manage a short flight. I pictured myself in a few hours, home with my family.

But my pep talk unraveled with each step toward the airplane gate. My heart began racing. My pulse quickened. I imagined the thrust of the jet's takeoff, jolts of turbulence in the sky, my stomach rising and falling at the dip of descent, and the bounce of landing. Feeling it all inside me at once, my legs became weak. I felt faint and helpless. I found a quiet corner, sat down, and texted my husband.

"I'm very dizzy. I don't think I can fly."

We had been trying for months to find an answer to my vertigo. It had ripped the rug from beneath daily life. Numerous times it left me and our kids stranded after I attempted to drive across town and then could not make it home. On bad days it was challenging to walk into a store without the walls skewing and bending inward on me.

> **Truly I tell you, whatever you did for one of the least of these brothers and sisters of mine, you did for me.**
>
> —MATTHEW 25:40 (NIV)

The past couple of weeks had been a reprieve, and I thought I could make this business trip happen. But there I was, huddled on an airport floor, terrified to board my plane.

My husband's response flashed across the screen of my phone.

"You need to find someone to help you."

I knew he was right. But I didn't know this airport or a soul within it. Loneliness ached deeply in my chest. Travelers whisked by with connections to catch. What do you do when you're completely vulnerable and needing help, but everyone seems preoccupied with their agendas?

Lord, show me who to talk to.

I wasn't convinced I could muster the courage to call on a stranger. But more and more, the prospect of stepping foot onto a plane was slipping from my staggering mind.

Making my way back toward the terminal entrance, I saw a woman in a security guard uniform. I'm not sure why, but I felt like I could talk to her.

"Excuse me," I said timidly. I caught her attention, and she turned to me.

"I'm sorry…It's just…My plane leaves in an hour. But…I'm really dizzy."

I wasn't sure what I was telling her or even what I was asking for. But it didn't seem to matter. Immediately her eyes softened and she jumped from her seat.

"We are going to take care of you," she assured me. Then she called her team through her radio.

We are going to take care of you. Help is always closer than it seems.

I am well familiar with the promise in Psalm 46:1 (NIV): "God is our refuge and strength, an ever-present help in trouble." However, I suppose I never realized how this help can arrive through the heart of a stranger.

I sat in her security point chair, my hands shaking and my head lowered to subdue the dizziness. A crowd passed quickly through the security checkpoint next to me, gathering laptops and shoes gliding down the belt and through the x-ray device.

The security woman turned back to me and laid her hand on my shoulder, then she began praying out loud over me. Right there in the airport, she called on the Spirit of God to calm, comfort, and protect me. The security gate became holy ground.

A team of paramedics arrived and gathered around me. They kindly created a wall with their bodies to block stares from curious travelers.

"Where are we going, sweetheart?" one asked me.

"The hospital, I guess." Tears pooled in my eyes, slipping down my face. "Oh, I mean Denver. I was going home."

The 900 miles separating me from my husband and kids felt like an endless chasm.

Someone came around the corner with a stretcher, and he gently helped me onto it. As they began wheeling me out of the airport and toward the waiting ambulance, the security woman broke through the crowd of paramedics to catch my gaze. She raised her hands, clasped together in front of her face, and mouthed, "I'm praying for you."

Show me who to talk to, I'd asked God. He did.

The kindness and prayers of this stranger carried me through the following frightening hours of blood tests, a CT scan, and the wait for my husband to arrive on the final flight of the night from Denver.

Praise be to the God and Father of our Lord Jesus Christ, the Father of compassion and the God of all comfort, who comforts us in all our troubles, so that we can comfort those in any trouble with the comfort we ourselves receive from God.

—2 CORINTHIANS 1:3–4 (NIV)

❧

Her words stayed with me in the coming months through doctor's visits, another stay in the emergency room, endless research, and finally, a diagnosis of vertical heterophoria. An ophthalmologist specializing in the disorder worked to dial in my prescription for prism glasses to correct my misaligned vision. In time I learned how to walk confidently, drive, and even fly on a plane again. Through each stage of the process, my mind traveled back to that frightening morning in the airport. I can hear the security guard's voice and feel her reassuring touch on my shoulder. I see her eyes. I feel her prayers.

Faith is powerful whether we know the faith-bearer or not. Prayer doesn't care whether we're well acquainted with the person praying or we've only collided with them in crisis. I spent fifteen minutes by the side of this woman, and her faith shifted my own.

"The LORD *is* near to all who call upon Him, to all who call upon Him in truth," Psalm 145:18 (NKJV) says. This woman was that "all" for me. When my thoughts were too frayed to piece together a coherent plea, she called on God on my behalf. My fragmented prayers felt isolated and alone, but she joined her unwavering faith to my struggling belief.

"We are going to take care of you," she'd promised. But it wasn't so much her radio call or the arrival of the paramedics that she was referring to. Instead, it was the genuine prayers and faith of a stranger, reminding me I am never alone.

From Hollywood
to Healing

By Mary Carlson as told to Shelly Beach

My childhood was an odd mix of ordinary and atypical, average
and unconventional. My sister, brother, and I were raised by
loving parents in the Chicago suburbs, and our stay-at-home
mom coordinated our household into our high school years.
Ours was a staunchly Catholic home, and I was committed
to the faith until I hit my mid-teens, when I took a class on
feminist perspectives at my Catholic high school that initiated a
feminist chapter in my story.

During my sophomore year at the College of St. Mary's of
Notre Dame, I participated in the Rome Program with other
students. Because of my less-than-wise actions on that trip, I
returned to the States. Looking for a fresh start, I enrolled at
San Diego State University, which wasn't far from Hollywood,
and changed my major to premed. I'd always had an interest in
healing and helping people who struggled with mental illness.
But during my premed studies, I learned that just a good GPA
wouldn't be enough to get me into med school.

A highly respected professor pulled me aside one day. "What
are you doing here?" he asked. "You can heal millions of people
making films."

While Mom was in many ways a typical at-home mom, our dad's job was less conventional. My parents met at the renowned Wilding Studios in Chicago, where Mom was a respected producer and Dad was an esteemed director. After they married and kids came along, my dad traveled half of the year directing movies. When we reached high school, Mom returned to work as an assistant director on shows like *Hill Street Blues*, *Chicago Story*, and independent movies.

> "But I will restore you to health and heal your wounds," declares the LORD.
>
> —JEREMIAH 30:17 (NIV)

Because of this I had naturally found my way into the movie business. I starred in my first commercial when I was seven years old. Dad produced new Ford and Lincoln Mercury commercials every year in California, and as I grew older, I went with him and learned to do script supervisor work. I then moved into television series, major motion pictures, commercials, and industry films. Eventually I found my niche as a script consultant.

However, my life wasn't sunshine and stardom. Growing up beside actors taught me to see "celebrities" like everyone else, as flawed and hurting people. My upbringing protected me from feeling intimidated or starstruck by others. And from the time I was a child, I learned to work hard.

I married the love of my life (I'll call him Bob), only to discover he suffered from horrifying childhood trauma. Despite his best intentions, he couldn't control his anger, addictions, and other destructive behaviors. I wanted to help him, but nothing worked. Our struggles caused me to call out to God for direction and purpose. I couldn't help Bob. Would God partner with me to bring the world hope?

Then one day an old friend called me—a woman I'd met a year or so before when I'd helped her fix her car that had broken down at the side of a road in Chicago. A mother of three, she'd been homeless at the time. Later, I gave Debra (not her real name) my car and introduced her to a business opportunity I thought might help her. I was surprised to hear her voice.

"I was volunteering at a church downtown when an author named Shelly Beach walked in. She was researching a novel and mentioned she wanted to get one of her other books made into a movie. I told her I had a friend who worked in the film industry and said you might give her a call."

I took the number from Debra, hung up, and didn't think about the call again for a week. Maybe two. But when I found Shelly's name and number deep inside the pocket of my jacket, I dialed the number.

Shelly answered and quickly gave me a summary of her book. I told her about a computer program that would help her format a screenplay and we chatted a while. Then the conversation shifted.

"Tell me about you, Mary," she asked. "I did a little research and found you listed as Mary Carlson and Mary Carlson Murphy. Which do you go by?"

I paused. I didn't really want to go into details about my divorce with a stranger.

"Mary Carlson. I married my husband—twice, actually. He had a terrible childhood, which made it a terrible marriage."

Shelly paused. "I'm guessing he may have experienced trauma and abuse like my best friend Wanda. I recently took her to intensive trauma treatment that changed her life in ten days. At fifty-five, she'd gone through every type of rehab and treatment. *Nothing* helped her. She didn't even know she had post-traumatic stress disorder (PTSD) until she met me. Therapists had been treating symptoms but not treating her PTSD for decades."

I couldn't believe what I was hearing.

"Wanda transformed more every day. We're so amazed and grateful, we can't stop talking about it. We now educate people about PTSD and the Instinctual Trauma Response method that saved Wanda's life."

I struggled to absorb what I'd heard. Trauma had destroyed Bob's life, and I'd battled beside him. Had God used a woman in a broken-down car to bring Shelly and her friend into my life to tell me about help for trauma and post-traumatic stress disorder—the mental illness that destroyed my husband's life and our marriage?

I shook my head in amazement. *This can only be a God-ordained triple connection from me to Debra, Shelly to Debra to me, and Shelly and Wanda with doctors who could treat her.*

Several weeks later, Shelly Beach and Wanda Sanchez waited eight hours to meet me at a restaurant in Illinois as I headed south to begin a new job on *Charlie's Angels.* As we talked about trauma, Shelly mentioned that Dr. Louis Tinnin and Dr. Linda Gantt, the founders of Intensive Trauma Therapy (ITT) (now Intensive Trauma Resolution ITR), were in frail health, and it would be wise to film their stories and therapy approach soon.

I left our meeting that night beyond dumbfounded.

Weeks before, just before "meeting" Shelly on the phone, I'd asked God to help me accomplish a task that would really help people.

We have to get this message out! had echoed throughout my thoughts as Shelly and Wanda had chatted with me. I understood how the brain operated, so I could see why the ITR approach to trauma resolution worked.

The day Shelly, Wanda, and I met at the restaurant, I became fascinated with Wanda's story of recovery from PTSD after her brief, intensive outpatient treatment. Before we left the restaurant that day, we planned a trip to the clinic in West Virginia, where I began to capture Dr. Lou and Dr. Linda on camera.

My goal quickly became to assist Dr. Lou and Dr. Linda to bring effective mental health healing to more people. I helped them transfer the power of their therapeutic approach to an app so people could work through healing on their own. I believe that helping those who cannot help themselves is what Jesus calls us to do.

> **He heals the brokenhearted and binds up their wounds.**
>
> —PSALM 147:3 (NIV)

The following five years flew by in a blur. I returned to West Virginia as often as possible to gather more footage of Lou and Linda (later just Linda after Lou died). Shelly and Wanda continued to advocate for the ITR treatment model and for greater understanding of mental health and trauma treatment. They launched PTSDPerspectives on Facebook.

Before long, my passion for mental health healing outweighed my job. Dr. Lou died suddenly of a heart attack, and Dr. Linda was diagnosed with cancer. I stopped working in television and movies and moved to West Virginia to care for

GOD'S GIFT OF TASTE

— By Lawrence W. Wilson —

"TASTE AND SEE that the LORD is good," the psalmist wrote (Psalm 34:8, NIV). But what does taste have to do with the character of God? Unlike sight, hearing, and smell, the sense of taste (like touch) depends on direct contact with the object of the experience. It is impossible to taste apples from a distance, though they may be seen. Fruit must be touched with the tongue, one of the most tender and sensitive and vulnerable parts of the body, to be tasted. That makes taste an apt metaphor for immersive experience, and especially applicable to a relationship with God.

Linda and help her transition the clinic to a stronger educational and online presence.

Today my vision and full-time work are helping people find healing from PTSD. Shelly and Wanda continue to support my work with Dr. Linda, and we offer counsel for their work with PTSDPerspectives and ongoing training opportunities. Our ongoing friendship feels more like sisterhood, and she continues her work with ITR as she maintains cancer treatment. I'm grateful God saw my kindred vision with Shelly, Wanda, and Linda long before we were born—to help people heal and become who God sees them to be.

Only God Has the Power to Heal

By Ellen Fannon

The day after Christmas 2004, the most destructive tsunami ever recorded occurred after a magnitude 9.1 underwater earthquake struck off the coast of Sumatra, Indonesia. Within fifteen minutes, the tsunami, measuring more than 100 feet, hit the west and north coasts of northern Sumatra, particularly devastating the heavily populated province of Aceh, known as the front porch of Mecca (the area with the strictest form of Islam). Entire communities were swept away in a matter of minutes. The death toll in Aceh was estimated at 150,000—half its population—with an additional several thousand people left homeless.

Not long after this, my husband and I were called to go help coordinate disaster relief efforts in Aceh. Having served two years with the Southern Baptist International Mission Board in Indonesia from 1999 to 2001, we were familiar with the culture and language. My husband also had extensive experience coordinating disaster relief during our two years in the field. We scraped together the money for plane tickets, put our lives on hold, and headed to the other side of the world.

One of the immediate needs was medical help for the many refugees. With a series of short-term volunteers, makeshift medical clinics were set up in mosques, refugee camps, and even by the side of the road. We worked in the heat, chaos, and primitive conditions, trying to bring a bit of hope and healing to a group of people who had lost everything. Word spread and soon we were asked to help in more remote areas.

On a Friday afternoon, our team journeyed deep into the jungle where there was a heavy concentration of GAM insurgents. The GAM was a separatist group seeking independence for Aceh from Indonesia. From 1976 to 2005, they fought against the Indonesian forces; more than 15,000 lives were lost in the conflict. We were a little uneasy but trusted that God had called us to this area for a reason and that He would protect us. We set up our clinic in an open area in front of one of the government buildings.

> **And the power of the Lord was with Jesus to heal the sick.**
>
> —LUKE 5:17 (NIV)

Our team ministered to numerous people that afternoon. During the busy clinic, many of our team members noticed a woman hovering on the periphery of the crowd, holding a sick baby. She didn't ask for help. Finally, when most of the people had gone and we were packing up to leave, she approached us, her eyes downcast. The baby in her arms was deathly ill. He was cyanotic (blue) and gasping for breath.

Among our team members that week were a pediatric emergency room nurse and a respiratory therapist. After examining the baby, they begged the mother to take him to the hospital, but she refused. Unfortunately, many hospitals in third-world countries have questionable standards of care. Patients' families must pay for everything up front, and unless a family member is continuously present, the patient may not receive any care.

With sinking hearts, realizing there was a good chance the baby would die, our nurse administered an antibiotic injection. Amazingly, we discovered one pediatric mask and one inhaler among our supplies. The mother was shown how to use the inhaler and to perform chest physiotherapy on the baby to loosen up congestion in his lungs. Finally, because we were finished for the day, the entire team had the opportunity to surround the mother and child, lay hands on them, and pray for healing in the name of Jesus. Our nurse and respiratory therapist planned to check on the baby the next day, so we took a picture of the mother and baby in order to find them again.

As we made the hour-long drive back into town, we realized the reason the mother had hung back until almost everyone else had gone. Most likely she was afraid we were going to tell her there was no hope for her child. The mood of our entire group was somber as we feared the worst.

The next day we received a phone call from our two volunteers who had gone back to check on the baby.

"It's a miracle!" they shouted. They were so excited it was hard to get the details. Finally, we learned they had taken the picture and gone through the village in search of the mother and baby. The villagers led them to a woman holding a smiling child.

"No, this isn't the same baby," they argued.

The people assured them it truly was the same child. It was nothing short of a miraculous healing!

After those ladies went back to the states, I journeyed out to the village several times to check on the baby. He was still on medication, but his recovery was astounding. I often ponder on the "coincidence" of having a respiratory therapist, an emergency room pediatric nurse, and one pediatric respiratory mask and inhaler in that remote jungle on that particular day. Coincidence? I think not. I believe God knew exactly what was needed for that critically ill baby and He provided. Although every healing is a blessing from God, whether it be cancer or a common cold, there was absolutely no doubt God's miraculous hand was on this baby.

> **And he took the children in his arms, placed his hands on them and blessed them.**
>
> —MARK 10:16 (NIV)

Our group was known as IBI (International Board Indonesia). We were nicknamed IB by the locals. Although there were several other secular humanitarian groups working in Aceh, we were told there was no healing until IB came.

"Doctors and medicines are simply tools. Only God has the power to heal." This is what we emphasized with each clinic we held. As I handed out medication and went over instructions, I prayed with each patient for healing in the name of Jesus. If someone had told me a year before that I would be standing in a mosque in the strictest Islamic area of Indonesia praying in the name of Jesus, I would have laughed.

I know that God can open doors in the most closed areas to receive His Gospel—and how He is still in the miracle business.

Widow or Window?

By Cookie Cranston

The August sun seared through the trees as the light crept across the silent room during the early morning. I experienced a level of silence I didn't even know existed. I poured a cup of my favorite dark roast coffee and placed it hesitantly on a coaster on the table. A stack of condolences waited to be acknowledged. A stack of forms needed to be filled out and returned. I had put it off for too many days. The official death certificates were tucked inside a lifeless brown envelope. Waiting. Waiting to make my husband's death official to parts of the universe that didn't know yet.

I fidgeted in the chair, my hands nervously gripping my elbows and wondering where to start with this dreaded task. I hadn't anticipated the associated anguish and trepidation. The death certificates would affix a stamp of finality. A finality for nearly every single thing that we had shared and that had been ours. Ours as a couple. Ours as a partnership and marriage. Ours as a team. Our dual identity.

Who exactly am I, alone without my soul mate? Part of me is gone. Nothing is "ours" now except our beautiful daughter. And just like that I'm no longer Mrs. I don't want to be Ms. There's a clear nod that Mrs. without the 'r' means something else. I don't want to be something else. I'm not divorced. I don't want to be single. And then there was the *W* word on the form glaring back at me too. *Oh, Father, please help me understand this.* That five-letter *W* word. The dialogue played repeatedly in my head, and at times I could barely hear my own thoughts over the piercing eerie silence that gripped me.

Though you have made me see troubles, many and bitter, you will restore my life again; from the depths of the earth you will again bring me up.

—PSALM 71:20 (NIV)

This new silence was contributing to the frustration and grim new outlook for my aloneness—the not-so-subtle gurgling of the coffee maker as it moved through its cycle; the *click* of the thermostat as it ticked through its own cycle, a *smack* not a *click* now; the rumble of a car on a once-quiet street; the shrill, seemingly boisterous voices of the songbirds, no longer the gentle chirps from their otherwise heavenly harmony. Almost annoying. The buzz of an ordinary day did not feel normal and natural. Oddly, in the stark stillness, typical sounds seemed to experience a sharp swell in volume. Sounds now felt loud and distracting in the deafening silence that persisted. My emotions were on the prickly surface, and my sensory perceptions seemed exaggerated.

I closed my eyes and slowly raised my quivering hands to cover my ears and whispered, "Heavenly Father, be with me in this moment. Be my strength as I begin to tackle all that I need to accomplish. Calm me. Let Your grace and peace touch me. Please, please be with me in this daunting solitary hour. You surely love me too much to leave me."

I slowly, deliberately slid my hands from my ears, briefly brushing my tear-moistened cheeks. Blurry eyed, I simultaneously reached for a tissue. I sighed, took a deep breath, followed with a slurp of tepid coffee. Would that be enough to numb me as I courageously lifted the first envelope off the pile marked, "Needs death certificate and obituary"?

The tears continued but I bravely opened the first trifolded piece of correspondence. The form appeared straightforward, not unlike many I had filled out at various times in my life— PLEASE PRINT: Name, address, telephone number, account number, date of birth, etc., followed by: CHECK ONE: Single, married, widowed, divorced. My index finger tapped nervously, strobe-like over the box next to WIDOW. At that very moment, it became hauntingly apparent that my life had changed forever. Breath gushed from my lungs and my head jerked forward to rest on my folded hands. My body felt rigid and limp at the very same time.

As an individual who loves and appreciates language and literature, I definitely have opinions about certain words and their uses—one of them being a complete aversion for the word *widow*. I had thoughts about that even as a young person, before I knew anything about anything. That word seemed such an unfair, perhaps even cryptic, mysterious label. As though it changed a person's identity somehow. Before the widow label, one would be a she, a Miss, a Ms., a Mrs., RN, Reverend, CPA, dog trainer, or a "hey you" even. But a widow? Who on this earth would want to be labeled and defined as a widow?

I felt I had little control over anything at this point, except perhaps my attitude and my identity. So in a quest for meaning and a sense of purpose, I researched the word *widow*, feeling certain that with the gazillion words in the English language there must be another word, a suitable replacement. A substitute. I looked up the origin—Indo-European—"be empty"; Sanskrit *vidh*—"be destitute"; Latin *viduus*—"bereft, widowed"; and Greek *eitheos*—"unmarried man." I looked for synonyms. I refused to check the widow box. I refused to be labeled empty, destitute, bereft, unmarried, and all the other would-be connotations that accompanied the word.

I even contacted a writer friend of mine who was writing a course for grieving widowed women. I expressed my obsession and disdain for the word *widow*. I mentioned my thoughts on it being such a cruel label on top of all the other issues for women who suddenly find themselves alone after the death of a spouse. She said it had never really come up before and that she really didn't know of another word.

Dead end. But by this time, I had dug in my heels.

I prayed about it relentlessly. I talked to God. I talked to myself about being rational about something I couldn't change, and still I was intent and concerned. I wasn't in denial, but I sure wasn't ready to be labeled a widow. I tried to convince myself that it didn't matter. But it did.

So, one day I sat with pen and paper just doodling. I wrote that word every which way. Finally, I wrote it in large, heavy letters in the middle of the page. Remember that game where you write down a word and then see how many words you can make with those letters? I stared at it intensely. Stubbornly. My Norwegianness shining through, I continued to stare.

It hit me like a lightning bolt—like a fresh serving of lefse, hot off the griddle. It had been staring at me the entire time. Add one beautiful little letter. A whole new word with a whole new meaning and a whole new world for this cookie. With the addition of an *n*, *widow* becomes *window*. So simple with such untold depth and meaning as well. And it wasn't just any word.

I had no idea who I was as a single woman—where to go, how to act, what to do with my time, with my life. After all, a part of me was gone forever. But having windows and becoming a window to the world of possibilities was exciting and liberating and reassuring. Above all, it was comforting.

> ## I can do all this through him who gives me strength.
>
> —PHILIPPIANS 4:13 (NIV)

I didn't know what was ahead for me or where I was going, but I knew the possibilities were endless and now felt empowered to move forward with God's help. People told me that eventually doors would open. I didn't even need doors now because in my heart and soul, I had windows in my wheelhouse. And I could literally see through them to envision new opportunities. And indeed, open them if I chose to do so. God is good.

When Forgiveness Is a Family Affair

By Anne George

My husband, Jason, and I were walking the Pacific shoreline and enjoying the gentle rhythm of the ocean waves against our legs when the call came. When I saw my brother Jim's number on my cell phone, panic rose in my chest. *Had Mom fallen? Did she wander away and get lost…or maybe have a low blood sugar event?*

Jim quickly reassured me nothing was wrong. No reason to panic; Mom was OK. But the words that came out of his mouth next stopped my heart.

"Susan and I need you to pack up all of Mom's things, Anne. We're not bringing her back to your house on Sunday. We've decided she'll be better off here with us…for the long term. We know you and Jason are trying, but we just don't think she's getting the care she needs in your home."

I stopped breathing. I couldn't have heard my brother right. *You and Susan don't think Jason and I are giving Mom the care she needs?* I stuttered the words back to him as I struggled to hold back the sobs gripping my throat.

"Anne, don't take this personally. We know you've done all you can and we're grateful, but we think it will be better for Mom here. You know, with Susan's nursing training and the kids here to help."

"Susan is sick and in bed most of the time," I responded to Jim through ragged breaths as Jason and I trudged back to the car through the beach sand. Tears were streaming down my cheeks. When Jason and I first learned that Mom was fighting Alzheimer's, we'd vowed that we'd take care of her until we were no longer able to do so. Susan and Jim had no right to simply take her from our home without a family discussion. And I didn't want to be unkind, but Susan had been nearly bedridden for the past several years. She certainly didn't need the pressure of her mother-in-law with Alzheimer's and her father-in-law with a heart condition moving into her home.

> **Hatred stirs old quarrels, but love overlooks insults.**
>
> —PROVERBS 10:12 (TLB)

But less than forty-eight hours later, Jim pulled out of our driveway with all of Mom's possessions piled in his van. I'd never felt so betrayed. And so heartbroken. I couldn't envision the empty days without my parents in the house. I'd given up my dream job as a paralegal to take care of my parents.

Mom had taken care of everyone around her all her life—people from church, friends with cancer, her sister, anyone in need. While other people bought missionary wives Tupperware when they came home on furlough, Mom bought them pretty lingerie because "They never buy luxuries for themselves, and they need to feel beautiful." She had a way of making everyone feel special.

Mom and Dad came in a set, like salt and pepper. My dad refused to leave her side out of pure devotion. Although he was a brilliant man who could converse on topics from economics to philosophy to biology, he was like a rudderless ship without my mom.

Having Dad move into my house when I was an adult was a bit challenging for me. He had a brusque way with words when I was a kid (and well into his older years), and I often found him to be rude and hurtful. Then, as an adult, I learned about his childhood and about people "on the spectrum" who struggle to understand human emotions, and a light dawned for me. Suddenly, my dad's actions made sense. I saw him with new eyes—as a man without the tools to unlock the secrets of human emotions, almost like a child. During the years Dad and Mom lived with Jason and me, I gained a deeper understanding of who he was and *why* he struggled to express emotions and show compassion.

Most importantly, I forgave my dad for the hurt I'd experienced because of his inability, and I committed to *show* him love and *tell* him I loved him at every opportunity, whether or not he said "I love you" in return. Little by little Dad began to change—in response to the changes I was making.

The man who'd never apologized to anyone began to say he was sorry—in quickly uttered phrases, but with genuine expressions of remorse. I soon found myself gently correcting him when he was rude and setting other healthy boundaries. And he began to respect what I asked of him. Childhood wounds began to heal, and I saw my dad with new compassion and insight.

Not long after Mom and Dad went to live with Jim and Susan, I realized that my parents had gone to live with them for reasons God understood and that I didn't have to comprehend. But my silent prayer became that Jim would experience deep father-son reconciliation with Dad before my father's death. When he was young, Jim had also been wounded by my father's emotional awkwardness.

My parents were blessed to live many precious years under the care of Jim and his family. Jason and I would often drive across the state to visit. We always found Mom and Dad surrounded by Jim and Susan's three adult children and grandchildren, who lived nearby. Dad was always holding a smiling baby, and Mom was always mesmerized by children playing around her or offering her their dolls or trucks.

When Mom's health began to decline, she and Dad moved into a dementia care facility a short distance from my brother's home and five minutes from their grandchildren. Dad didn't have dementia, but he refused to be separated from her. My mother passed away surrounded by family who loved and cherished her. At the end of her life, she was surrounded by children, grandchildren, and great-grandchildren who sang her favorite hymns and whispered her favorite stories from past family gatherings.

> **Bear with each other and forgive one another if any of you has a grievance against someone. Forgive as the Lord forgave you.**
>
> **—COLOSSIANS 3:13 (NIV)**

And when my father was called to heaven six years later, he and my brother were alone in Dad's hospital room as his strength slipped away, as God had planned my dad's homegoing before time. Father and son and Father and Son were together for one final moment of healing after the exchange of prayers and memories and shared hearts and silence, when words are no more and heaven touches earth.

Hidden Purposes

By Eric Wilfredo Santos as told to Wanda Sanchez

According to my mother, I was just two when the trouble started. Of course, I don't remember, but by the time I was four, my young spirit witnessed what true faith looked like. I like to call this unremembered time in life the beginning of my "incredible journey."

Ours wasn't a household of faith, as some people describe their homes. My parents were born in El Salvador and came to the United States in their teens. Dad was an atheist until shortly before he died at sixty-six, and if someone asked Mom about religion, she said she was Catholic. I did have a praying grandmother, and that explains a lot.

It was a brisk November day in the City by the Bay, San Francisco, California, when I arrived and claimed my place in the world, the fifth son of six. My mom says I was a healthy, inquisitive, energetic little guy.

Until one day I wasn't.

I was two years old when I began to urinate blood. Concerned, my parents immediately made an appointment with my pediatrician at Kaiser Hospital in San Francisco. The doctor's office door barely closed before my mother began to voice her concerns about my health. After asking my mom questions to assess my problem, Mom acknowledged that she *had* given me red Kool-Aid with lunch. The doctor discounted my discolored urine as an anomaly caused by the sugary beverage and sent me home. With my mother, of course.

A few days later, red-tinged urine appeared again. This time my mother proactively took a specimen in a jar directly to the doctor. Seeing the discoloration, he confirmed that it looked like blood and sent the specimen for testing.

Next, I was scheduled to see a nephrologist who saw "evidence" that prompted my visit to the dimly lit bowels of the hospital for x-rays. Shadowed areas in my kidney caused concern about a potentially bigger, more complex problem. After intense discussions with my parents, the surgeon decided to proceed with exploratory surgery. The goal was to see if the problem was with my kidney or something else.

My right kidney was removed that evening, and when lab results came back, the mass was identified as Wilms' tumor, a rare kidney cancer that typically affects children. Also known as nephroblastoma, it's the most common kidney cancer in children. Wilms' tumor typically affects children between the ages of three and four. It often appears in just one kidney, although it sometimes is found in both kidneys simultaneously.

> **Many are the plans in a person's heart, but it is the LORD's purpose that prevails.**
>
> —PROVERBS 19:21 (NIV)

The year passed quickly, and, according to my mother, my recovery went well. My radiation treatment involved frequent trips to two different hospitals and caused muscle loss and severe scarring of my abdomen. My prescription?

Healthy living. By the time I was three, Mom had given birth to brother number six, and life was getting back to normal, meaning my cancer was no longer the driving force in our family.

I was three and a half when I went to a follow-up appointment that revealed a large mass on my remaining left kidney. The doctors matter-of-factly laid out the frightening prognosis to my parents. If the mass was cancer, my days would be numbered. The devastating report took its toll, and shortly after this news, my parents divorced. My mother carried a heavy burden during those days—raising six sons alone was a numbing responsibility. No matter how hard she tried to hide her distress, I always saw it.

Mom had always worked—now, three jobs. At one point she worked at a Marriott commercial kitchen loading a conveyor belt. While at her job one day, a colleague who worked across from her asked if she was OK.

"Every day at work I watch you," her coworker replied. "You always work hard, but you look so sad, so heartbroken. What's causing you such despair?"

Stifling her sobs, my mother nodded.

"My husband and I split up, so I'm raising six boys on my own. The youngest is two, and my four-year-old has cancer. The doctors say he won't see his next birthday. I'm scared."

Through her tears, my mother quietly told the woman about my health. Her coworker leaned in, listening intently.

"I don't know what you believe, but there's a man in my church that the Lord uses in mighty ways. Can I bring him to your house to pray with you for your boy?" Before this woman could finish her question, my mother had scheduled the visit. Since my illness, my mother's interest in God had stirred to life.

The night the knock came at the door, I answered. It seemed like I was looking up for a very long time before I finally saw the man's face. *He must be a giant,* I remember thinking. The mysterious, hatted stranger was accompanied by two women, one standing on either side of him. I vividly remember that he smelled good and was holding a briefcase.

We went into the living room, and I sat on the couch near my mom. As the mystery man popped the sliding latches on his case, he took a small glass vial filled with anointing oil and spoke to me in Spanish.

"Son, I'm going to pray to the Lord on your behalf. If I get a little loud, don't get scared, OK?"

He put one hand on the crown of my head, and with a finger of his other hand, he put oil on my forehead. Then he started praying in Spanish in a thunderous, vibrato voice that bombarded heaven and beseeched God for my healing. I'm sure I heard the windows rattle with the power in his voice.

My eyes were closed, but I could smell his cologne. Then suddenly I had the most beautiful experience of my life. I remember that moment as if it happened yesterday, but I still struggle to find words to describe what happened. Something powerful, like electricity, filled my body. My hands stretched open, and I felt the most incredible peace as my sense of time melted away.

When I opened my eyes, my mom was crying joyful tears. I ran to her and asked if she'd felt it. I asked the Church Man if he'd felt it too. He smiled and said, "Yes, son, I felt it."

Later that week I had an appointment at Kaiser Hospital for more x-rays and an appointment with an oncologist in San Francisco. The doctor sat across from my mother and softly mumbled, before finally saying that the mass they'd once seen on earlier x-rays was gone. He couldn't explain it. I know that God healed me because He had a purpose for my life.

Today I'm in my fiftieth year of borrowed life from my Creator. He's protected me as He promised in His Word. I've volunteered serving inmates in the San Francisco county jail and shared the gospel with those doing their time in prison three times a week for more than twelve years. I've prayed for, encouraged, loved, and cried with men who had to be locked up to be set free! And God has sent me into El Salvador's prisons to film the stories of hardened criminals who have come to Christ and started their own ministries. Praise God!

I've also worked at a Christian radio network and was hired at secular ABC Radio, sharing the gospel on air. I'm now retired from radio, but never from service to the Lord. I recently wrote and directed my first award-winning feature film, *Cheo*, which can be seen on digital platforms like Xfinity On Demand, Amazon Prime, and ChristianCinema.com. Once again, God fulfilled His purpose and allowed me to share His story through yet another avenue.

> ## I cry out to God Most High, to God, who vindicates me.
>
> —PSALM 57:2 (NIV)

God spared my ordinary life so I could share His message in everyday life and beyond—on the radio, through movies and media connections, and in jails and prisons to accomplish His extraordinary purposes—introducing people to Him.

But isn't that just like Jesus?

GOD'S GIFT OF SMELL

— By Lawrence W. Wilson —

THERE'S NOTHING QUITE like the aroma of fresh-brewed coffee or lilacs in the springtime. The human nose has some 400 scent receptors and can detect up to 1 trillion smells, according to scientific studies. Yet we don't begin to absorb the infinite variety of scent in our world. Dogs have up to 300 million olfactory receptors. Our canine companions can detect the unique scent of a human being, even the presence of diseases like cancer. Spices, chocolate chip cookies, ocean breezes—when the human nose has enjoyed every good scent to its fullest capacity, there is still more to experience.

God of the Snowdrifts

By David L. Winters

Waking up from the anesthetic, I had trouble focusing on the man just inches from my face. I recognized my surgeon from earlier in the morning. He'd promised to fix my knee and get me back on the tennis court by spring. Now, his garbled phrases ran together as my brain languished between sleep and waking. After an apparently long pause, he asked if I had any questions.

"Only one," I said, struggling through the mental fog. "How did the operation go?"

His reaction indicated he'd just explained the whole thing. I'd been too woozy to comprehend my debriefing.

"Oh, you aren't out of the anesthetic yet," he said in a voice that sounded disappointed and accusatory. He must have felt like he'd just wasted his time.

"We can talk more in my office at your follow-up appointment in a few days."

The doctor had successfully repaired my torn meniscus and cleaned up the arthritis in my knee. Just a few hours after waking up from the operation, a friend drove me home. A giant bandage circled my leg several times.

An avid recreational tennis player, I'd made it through a host of sports injuries and two carpal tunnel surgeries without post-op prescription drugs. God would see me through this time as well, I was sure.

With a snowstorm forecast for later in the week, I'd stock-piled a collection of canned soups and sandwich meats. Dozens of books called to me from my "to-read" pile. Frankly, I probably needed a break from my busy life. My plan included a week of recovery before heading back to work at the Department of Homeland Security.

One major problem with this single man was that I prided myself on being self-reliant, even in challenging situations. Despite offers from church friends to bring me "a casserole or two," I steadfastly declined and resolved to make do on my own.

Recovery day one passed quickly. When the surgery medications wore off overnight, I woke with tenderness in my knee that gave way to throbbing by midmorning. I took one of the prescription pain-killers and slept through most of the afternoon and night.

> And those who know Your name will put their trust in You; For You, LORD, have not forsaken those who seek You.
>
> —PSALM 9:10 (NKJV)

On the second day, I woke up feeling lonely and vulnerable. Although my knee remained heavily bandaged, my imagination envisioned enflamed incision sites and massive swelling. Fear and self-pity tried to invade my recovery. Experience told me I needed an infusion of God's Word.

I gathered my favorite morning beverage and limped to the kitchen table. I opened my Bible and read the beginning of the second book of Timothy until the following verse jumped off the page: "For God has not given us a spirit of fear, but of power and of love and of a sound mind" (2 Timothy 1:7, NKJV). God's presence filled my heart with assurance of His loving care. My anxiety began to dissipate. Loneliness remained, but I asked God to relieve it and continue healing my leg. When my quiet time concluded, I gingerly made my way to my recliner in the living room, perhaps to find an old movie or television program on cable. Little did I know how God would answer my prayer.

My neighbor Janice, a single mom, had sometimes asked me to pick up her children from school. This family has been a huge blessing to me, occasionally including me in meals, birthday parties, and other activities. She called with a minor emergency, asking if I could pick up her daughter Cindy from school. Having done so in previous minor emergencies, I knew the way to Cindy's school and where to retrieve her. Without thoroughly thinking through the situation with my knee, I agreed to pick her up and ended the call.

God, I implored, *You see the situation. Help me get to the school and back safely.* After donning oversized sweatpants and my coat, it was time for an adventure.

I opened the front door to a winter scene enveloping my front yard. Already several inches of snow covered the front steps. I carefully descended the stairs and walkway to the curb. It would take several minutes to brush off the wet flakes from the car windows. I remember thinking this wasn't the smartest thing I'd ever done. What else could I do? A child was waiting at school and the roads weren't getting any better.

There was a layer of ice under the snow, which I discovered as my car slid a bit at the first stop sign. I plodded along until I finally turned into the school's driveway. The trip to Cindy's school usually takes twenty minutes. In the blizzard-like conditions, it took double that amount of time. Cindy waved from under the main portico, clutching her beloved sousaphone.

"Just put your instrument in the back seat," I said as she opened the passenger-side door.

"OK, Mr. Winters."

Cindy was a great kid. I'd watched her grow up since I moved next door to her family almost ten years earlier. Good-natured and full of energy, she often chatted me up over the fence as I tended my garden. Her endless stories made the gardening go quickly.

"This snow is something," I said. "Didn't know it would come on so quickly."

"Yeah, my band practice got canceled at the last minute," Cindy said. "Thanks for picking me up."

"Sorry it took me so long to get here. The roads are jammed. It will take extra time, but we'll get home safely. Your mom will no doubt be late as well."

We started for home and encountered trouble almost immediately. The snarled traffic translated into a long wait to even get back onto the main road. Cindy made small talk and affirmed her appreciation for the warm car ride home.

After one of many prayers, I was let out of the school's driveway by a kind driver. I soon saw the reason for the long string of cars. A treacherous, icy hill proved a major obstacle for drivers ahead of us. As we stopped on the hill, a sports car just ahead of us spun its wheels. I wondered if it might slide back into us, but God protected us.

My usually sure-footed Chevy began to slide backward a little at the next pause on the hill.

"God help us!" Cindy shouted. Her fervent prayer received an instant answer as the tires gripped and we stopped before sliding into the compact car in my rearview mirror.

I felt an internal tug to quote the following scripture for both Cindy's benefit and my own: "There is no fear in love; but perfect love casts out fear, because fear involves torment. But he who fears has not been made perfect in love" (1 John 4:18, NKJV).

> **Cast your cares on the LORD and he will sustain you; he will never let the righteous be shaken.**
>
> —PSALM 55:22 (NIV)

For the next ninety minutes, cars crawled through the worsening conditions as large flakes descended all around. Though a beautiful scene, both Cindy and I wished our journey would end soon. So did her mom. In all, Janice called Cindy six times.

I eventually turned off the main avenue into our familiar neighborhood. We didn't get far until my car began to hang up in the rising snow. I could see the writing on the wall and maneuvered for the curb. We parked, still almost a mile from our homes.

"Cindy, it looks like we will have to walk from here. You can leave your sousaphone in the car if you want."

"I better carry it. My mom paid a lot to buy it for me, and I don't want it to freeze."

I prayed for my knee. Nowhere in the rehabilitation planning sheet did my doctor recommend walking a mile in two- and three-foot snowdrifts this soon after surgery. Yet, there I

GOD'S GIFT OF HEARING
— By Eryn Lynum —

WALKING BESIDE A frozen lake on a winter night, one can experience an eerie and intriguing symphony. As water freezes and expands, a mysterious and echoing *pop* splits open the silence. Pressure in the ice builds up, creating cracks and sending loud punctuations into an otherwise calm evening. God's limitless love can have a similar effect on the hearts of His children. His love swells in one's spirit, sometimes cracking previous boundaries to create new thresholds. Sudden growing pains may be a sign of a new capacity for His grace in one's heart.

---

went, plodding away with Cindy and her sousaphone in tow. After a few blocks, Cindy began dragging the heavy sousaphone case on top of the snow.

"Cindy, I better take the sousaphone for a while," I said.

"But your knee..." she protested.

"My leg's doing fine. Let's just keep walking and get home."

Finally, we made it to Cindy's house. She took the giant case from me and climbed the steps to her front door. She thanked me and disappeared into the two-story Cape Cod.

After getting inside my own warm home, I offered thanks to the Lord. My pants and bandages were soaked through, but I made it safely. In the days to come, my leg healed quickly, and I returned to work. The walk in the snow caused no obvious complications. As promised by my surgeon, I began playing tennis again in my spring league. God proved himself king of all my circumstances, even three-foot snowdrifts.

A Running Miracle

By Mindi Schrock as told to Shelly Beach

Surgery days were always the same. My husband, Brad, and I stood at the intake desk, asking and answering the usual questions, then receiving and checking medical bracelets and signing medical forms. As usual, we'd slung backpacks stuffed with water and juice bottles, snacks, pajamas, phones, chargers, *real* tissues, Brielle's medical journal, her favorite blanket, a Bible, and M&Ms over our shoulders. Brad carried Brielle's sister in his arms. She also came to us with complex medical problems, but this time wouldn't be her turn. Finally, Brielle's name was called for surgery prep (*this* time it was Brielle, not Natalie, undergoing surgery).

Brad and I had arrived before dawn that morning. Our daughter Brielle was the first surgery of the day. Time would eventually teach us that doctors schedule their more difficult cases early in the day. We felt peace as we sat quietly reading books to our daughter. God had given us peace and strength I cannot explain from our very first decision to adopt our two little girls.

Looking back now from the vantage point of nearly five years with our daughters, I see that God must have perceived strengths and abilities in Brad and me that we had no idea we possessed. We knew our adoption journey would be difficult, but that concept was void of experience. We were ordinary parents with two relatively healthy boys and had never sat vigil

at a child's bedside or paced a surgical waiting room anticipating an outcome. I had never seen myself as a mother of a
special needs child with a cape of wisdom and Kryptonite faith.

Our last two months had flown by in a blur. Brad and I
had adopted our two three-year-old daughters from China on
August 17, 2017, barely seven weeks before. Brielle's surgery
had been scheduled on October 3, not even five weeks after
her first cardiology appointment. Our daughter desperately
needed open heart surgery for a hole in her heart and Tetralogy
of Fallot, a very rare heart
condition caused by a combination of four heart defects
that are present at birth.

Brielle's adoption file had
stated that she had a heart
condition, but it also said she
had no symptoms. We had her
file reviewed and knew she
would need surgery, but if she
was not showing symptoms,

> **But You, O LORD,
> are a shield about
> me, my glory, and
> the lifter of my head.**
>
> —PSALM 3:3 (ESV)

how sick could she be? We determined that we really couldn't
know how sick she was until she arrived, so we prayed as we
waited for her arrival.

We observed symptoms in Brielle's first few weeks with us.
She was always tired. Her color wasn't right. Was it just from
her lack of nutrition? But then one day, a week after our return
home from China, her fingers turned blue. We immediately recognized that our daughter needed to see a cardiologist. And fast!

As parents, we faced a potential crisis. Brad and I had never
needed a pediatric cardiologist before. We weren't "connected"
in the pediatric health community. But God knew our need.

He'd already paved the way through a connection I'd made with a fellow adoptive mama warrior with a child with a heart problem. We were scheduled immediately to meet with a world-renowned pediatric cardiac specialist.

"Think about it," he said to us. "All this time she's been thriving without any medical reason—and without seeing a cardiologist."

I was puzzled. I didn't understand what he meant because I didn't yet understand how dire Brielle's heart condition was. Perhaps God was protecting me from that knowledge. I do remember the doctor going over the potential outcomes of the surgery. All of them. When he started reviewing the worst possible scenarios, I stopped him as I raised my hand.

"I have peace."

"No," he urged me. "You don't understand. Let me explain again. It's possible that—"

I shook my head. "No. I *do* understand. I'll listen to what you have to say, but I have peace. Whatever the outcome, it was meant to be. I also know she'll be OK. I just know."

The look in his eyes said he needed to prepare Brad and me for the worst. I probably wasn't prepared for the worst. Who can ever be? The doctor explained the possible outcomes again, and I nodded with a quiet smile, then thanked him.

With a look of resignation, he selected a surgery date.

"That's just over a month away…Can we wait?"

I saw in his eyes that my question told him I had no idea the dangers in the upcoming battle.

"Let's get this done before the weather gets bad," he said compassionately, giving me an "out" to continue in my denial and pretend everything was going to be fine. He didn't explain that Brielle was a rare emergency high-risk case. He chose to be gentle.

But I knew. I saw the truth in his eyes—maybe not to the extent he wanted me to know, but I knew. But knowing did not disturb my peace. I *knew* Brielle was going to be OK. And I knew Brad and I had to be OK for her—despite the chaos or complications.

So we scheduled the surgery and went home to rest. I was feeling rather sick and run-down. Did I mention that the day before we scheduled surgery, I'd been diagnosed with pneumonia?

Now, here we were, finally at surgery day.

We took pictures, talked to the all the nurses, doctors, and anesthesiologists, and then Brielle was ready. We hugged her and told her we'd be there when she woke up. She'd been home from China just seven weeks and had no idea what we were saying when we spoke to her, but she could sense we were at peace.

Brad and I settled into the waiting area and scheduled meals and potential breaks. The surgery would last five to six hours, so we had to pace ourselves. It was torture to sit and wait. I had to walk. I had to go get coffee. I had to move.

Updates were few and far between.

Brielle was doing fine.

She was breathing well.

This part of the surgery was complete.

They have moved onto the *next*.

I walked and paced the hospital and went outside for fresh air. I forced myself to stay busy. Sitting and waiting meant sitting and worrying.

Then, unexpectedly, the surgery nurse came in the late afternoon and gave a final report. Brielle's surgery was done, and she would soon be heading to recovery. My hands began to shake, and I inhaled deeply as I anticipated the report.

The doctor walked into the room and pulled off his mask. I tried to read his face.

"Brielle did great. We repaired everything as planned. However, the hole was bigger than I expected."

He showed us an image of her heart and the patch they'd used to repair the hole, then pointed at a piece of odd fabric the nurse had handed me. A section about the size of a quarter was cut out of the material.

"Your daughter's heart is about the size of a large strawberry," the nurse told me.

I stared at the patch hole again.

The nurse started to walk away, and I reached out and stopped her.

"How was Brielle able to run with a hole that big in her tiny heart?"

"We have no medical explanation." She smiled slightly and walked back toward the surgery doors.

Brad and I stared at each other in shock. We examined the material and the hole again, dumbfounded by what we saw—a miracle! Our daughter Brielle *was* and *is* a walking, running miracle!

Brad and I hugged each other and went to see our girl in recovery, then the ICU. Her skin color was noticeably improved. And although she was weak and disoriented from surgery, she still appeared strong.

Over the course of her recovery, Brielle was tough. She ate and walked sooner and faster than most other children who were recovering. She amazed the doctors and nurses with how quickly she rebounded. Before we knew it, she was ready to go home.

Our adoption story has also included heartache, tears, and trauma. We've faced unexpected battles that have drained our spiritual, physical, and emotional resources, but God has never left our side. He's helping us not only mold the lives of our two older boys, but He's also helping us reclaim the physical bodies, emotions, spirits, and souls of two small girls from China—an extraordinary task that we can only do through the power of His name.

> **It is the LORD who goes before you. He will be with you; he will not leave you or forsake you. Do not fear or be dismayed.**
>
> **—DEUTERONOMY 31:8 (ESV)**

Through our adoption journey, God has given us peace and strength we can't explain. And two of His children who are surviving to the glory of His name.

Greatness comes by doing a few small and smart things each and every day. Comes from taking little steps, consistently. Comes from a making a few small chips against everything in your professional and personal life that is ordinary, so that a day eventually arrives when all that's left is The Extraordinary.

—Robin Sharma, author

CHAPTER 5

God's Gift of Second Chances

A Housewife with a Hobby

By Mary Potter Kenyon

I stood in front of the closed doors of the conference center, steeling myself to enter. I was fifty-one years old, a stay-at-home mother who'd maintained writing as a creative outlet as she raised eight children. Despite having published over 500 pieces, I was certain I didn't belong in a room full of "real" writers.

Being bullied mercilessly as a child had battered my self-esteem. Years of isolation as a homeschooling mother living in the country had resulted in my lack of a single friendship outside of my husband and sisters, along with an inability to string two sentences together to talk to anyone beyond the butcher and the mailman. I'd spent the previous two years failing to sell a completed book manuscript and lost all confidence in myself as a writer. I truly didn't see myself as anything more than a housewife with a hobby.

But your mother believed in you. And so does your husband, I reminded myself as I pushed open the door and entered. In fact, my mother's death a few months before had prompted me to register for the event. If Mom could face a terminal diagnosis of cancer with courage and grace, I could brave a Christian writing conference for the first time. My husband, David, had · insisted I attend, offering to watch our children for three days.

I was pleasantly surprised by the warm welcome I received from the group of writers, although I was initially skeptical of the sincerity of women and men who talked about God like He was their friend and how He'd guided them in their writing and life.

Why didn't God talk to me? I wondered.

I left the conference with something I'd never managed to cultivate as an adult: several fledgling friendships, along with a desire for the personal relationship these new friends had with their Savior.

I would need those friends and my new relationship with God a few months later when David, a five-year cancer survivor, unexpectedly died following a heart stent surgery. I was widowed at the age of fifty-two, with four of my eight children—ages eight, twelve, fifteen, and eighteen—still at home. The rote prayers of my childhood suddenly seemed insufficient. Instead, I craved the kind of conversational prayer I'd seen at the writing conference. Thrust into a state of stillness through mourning, I began each day with solitude, reading the Bible and praying like I'd never prayed before. I was searching for answers that came in the unaccustomed silence of a house emptied of a life partner.

> **So do not throw away your confidence; it will be richly rewarded.**
>
> **—HEBREWS 10:35 (NIV)**

Not long after David's death, I began to write about my grief as a way of processing my pain. My new friends from the conference encouraged me when I began to receive invitations to speak in churches, libraries, and other venues around the state. Little did I know that they were observing my abilities to connect with my audience and effectively communicate my material while speaking from my heart.

I was invited to speak at that next year's conference. Following my morning presentation, I attended a media promotion workshop conducted by two professionals in writing and publishing.

"Who would be your ideal radio guest?" someone asked Wanda, who was responsible for booking guests for a major radio program. We all leaned forward to hear the answer. Surely it would be someone famous.

"Mary Potter Kenyon." If she hadn't looked right at me, I'd have thought I'd misheard. "She's knowledgeable, enthusiastic, and articulate," she continued. "After hearing her this morning, I would say Mary would be the perfect radio guest." Wanda's colleague, Shelly, nodded in assent. My eyes darted nervously from one to the other, waiting for the punch line. Instead of amusement, I saw pride in their eyes, and something else—love.

The rest of the workshop was a blur. As soon as it concluded, I grabbed my purse and bolted for the car. There was no way I could stay for the remaining presentations that day. My legs felt weak, and my hands were shaking. I started crying even before I turned the key in the ignition.

Were these two media professionals serious? I wondered as I drove in the direction of my house an hour away. *Me, the perfect radio show guest? A woman who just a year before could barely talk to strangers. Articulate?*

I pondered these things as I drove toward home, swiping steadily flowing tears from my cheeks. I was reminded of a conversation I'd had with David just weeks before he died. We were on the couch, watching a powerful female speaker on television. When she mentioned how often she went to her hairdresser to keep her hair looking nice, my husband turned to me and said, "You're going to be like her someday. I want you to get your hair done whenever you need to, for your public."

I'd been flabbergasted. My husband saw *me* as a powerful speaker? *With a public following?*

Hardly a public speaker, I'd just begun conducting beginning writing workshops two months before. David had been present the first time I did a workshop. "I love seeing you come alive in front of a room. You're made for this," he'd commented afterward with the same look I'd just seen in Wanda and Shelly's eyes.

I was crying so hard by this time that I had to pull off the road, overcome by emotion and a revelation: *David had seen something in me. Wanda and Shelly saw something in me.*

I considered how I'd felt that morning, conducting the workshop. I'd never felt more alive. For that brief hour, I'd forgotten I was a newly widowed mother. Was that a sign I was doing what God had planned for me? Could He have designed me for a ministry of public speaking?

I pondered the Bible verse I'd written in my journal shortly after David died, the one I continually referred to in the weeks and months of early grieving: "For I know the plans I have for you," declares the LORD, "plans to prosper you and not to harm you, plans to give you hope and a future" (Jeremiah 29:11, NIV).

At best, I'd been a lukewarm Christian before my husband's death, praying but never having learned to discern God's voice. After David's death, by turning to prayer and the Bible, I'd managed to develop the personal relationship with Jesus I'd yearned for the year before.

I saw then how God had prepared me for the loss of my husband in the months preceding his death. I clung to God's promise that there was a future for me after the death of my husband. The verse suddenly took on new meaning in light of what I heard from Wanda and Shelly, who would become my mentors.

Slowly it dawned on me and fresh sobs escaped my lips with new certainty: God did, indeed, have plans for me beyond the writing I'd been doing.

> **For the Spirit God gave us does not make us timid, but gives us power, love, and self-discipline.**
>
> —2 TIMOTHY 1:7 (NIV)

My world became bigger after that realization. I discovered a sense of purpose in my broken self, laid bare by grief. A few months later, I signed a contract for the book I'd attempted to sell for nearly two years. I would go on to write and sell six more books in the ensuing seven years. I began speaking on finding hope in grief and took online courses to become a certified grief counselor, founding an annual grief retreat in 2016. Those initial writing workshops turned into programs on grief, expressive writing, and creativity. Public speaking on those same topics became a passion with purpose, as I began to encourage and inspire other women in their own creativity.

I am convinced that none of it—not the books, the speaking opportunities, or even the counseling certificate—would have been possible on my own. All credit goes to God. Only He could equip a "housewife with a hobby" for something much more, fulfilling His design for her life.

Healed Feet and Hearts

By Mindi Schrock

June 14, 2019, is forever etched in my memory as a "line in the sand" life-shifting day for me.

It began with great expectations. I dropped off my two five-year-old medically fragile daughters at respite care for the weekend. My eleven- and thirteen-year-old sons and I had planned a wonderful day, starting with a hike at Warren Dunes State Park. We'd just arrived at the entrance when I received a text from my husband, Brad.

"I fell off a ladder and broke my ankle. I'm in the ER waiting for tests."

I thought for a moment, then texted a question. "Could we go for a quick hike, then come?"

My conscience twinged as I typed. Medical issues always pushed the boys to the side, and the injury didn't sound bad. Brad would understand I didn't want to nix their outing for another trip to the ER.

Brad agreed, so the boys and I set out on a short hike. But a few minutes later, I received a second text. "The right ankle is crushed, and the left Achilles is torn."

Reality hit me.

"Boys, we need to go," I called as I turned back toward the car. I quickly posted an update on Facebook, asking for prayers. Just hours before, I'd written an upbeat post about our family's first respite break in almost two years since we'd adopted the girls and how much we needed it.

Now this. How…ironic.

At the hospital, the doctors' words flew so fast I could barely process them—admitted, surgeries, care plan, wheelchair.

Trust in the LORD forever, for the LORD, the LORD himself, is the Rock eternal.

—ISAIAH 26:4 (NIV)

But it's only injured feet, Lord. We need this time to rest from the girls' challenges and the toll they've taken on our lives.

I headed home with my sons, who needed to eat and sleep, medical terminology flooding my mind. Then I turned around and went back to the hospital with necessities for Brad. As I drove home alone later, I could barely see through my tears.

My thoughts swirled as I took a hot shower and cried.

How am I going to do this, God?

I'd never felt so alone. Brad's first surgery was to be Saturday morning, the day of our son's playoff baseball game. How could I be present for Brad's surgery *and* Graham's game? I'd have to miss Graham's game.

Again, I sobbed. *I'd have to tell the coach again that Graham wouldn't have a parent at his game, and once again he wouldn't have the support he deserved.*

Brad's second surgery was scheduled for Monday. I was supposed to pick up the girls from respite care on Sunday afternoon. What was I going to do with them while I was at the hospital? Both of our families had probably found out about Brad's injury through my Facebook post. I couldn't deal with my emotions about Brad's injuries *and* worry about family relationships. I felt like my husband and I had no one to support us—only Jesus and each other. With our girls' medical and emotional needs, our family was too heavy a burden for most people, including our extended families.

We'd adopted our girls two years earlier. Both had chronic complex medical needs that required multiple surgeries and ongoing treatment.

And Brad and I always cared for the girls as a team. Together.

I sobbed as the water poured over me. I'm not sure how long I'd been crying in the shower when I heard God's voice speak quietly, deep in my soul. "Mindi, I protected him."

How? He's hurt.

"I covered him. The Enemy's plan was death, is always death. I covered him so only his feet were injured, and his life was spared."

A picture flashed in my mind, and I saw an angel covering Brad as he lay on the ground. Covering all but his feet.

But why, God? Why his feet?

Silence…

I can't do this, God, I need help! I must be at the hospital on Monday for his surgery. I can't leave the kids home alone—especially the girls. I must be with Brad during surgery. God, show me what to do!

I searched my mind for anyone I could call. Our daughters' special care had intensified already strained family relationships. In the past, my parents had been reluctant to help with the girls' complex medical needs. I couldn't ask them now.

I'm on my own, I told myself, *but not alone. God, help me.*

Unknown to me, my mom had read my Facebook post and texted me. Afraid to trust her with my pain, I sent a quick reply, trying to brush her off with facts and medical information. Nothing personal, just data.

The next morning someone picked Graham up to go to his baseball game. (I think it was his coach.) I was heartbroken to miss another of Graham's events and sad that Brad had to miss it too. Brad's dad was there when I arrived at the hospital, but he quickly left. So, Brad and I faced his surgery alone, like so many other challenges in past years. None of us seemed to know how to start moving beyond our hurts.

The surgeon found me after surgery. He talked about insurance, then tackled the treatment plan that sounded like the post-surgery reports I'd heard following the girls' medical procedures. But this time Brad was responsible for implementing the plan himself. Our oldest son Peyton was there, but I didn't want him to take responsibility, so I took responsibility for the treatment plan.

My stomach sank as I made decisions *for* Brad, instead of *with* Brad.

I kept it together as I spoke with the doctor about what I should expect because that's what I do—hold it together until I fall apart.

Another surgery on Monday. Several days in the hospital. Moving to rehab or setting up a hospital room at home. Six-month recovery, including three to four months in a wheelchair. I struggled to process the words: care plan, hospital bed, ramps, bathroom/shower needs, wheelchair. *Were our hallways even wide enough for a wheelchair?*

As my mind spun, I got a text from my mom. "Is there anything we can do?"

Pause. *Had I read right?*

"Do you want us to come?"

Stunned hesitation. "Yes."

"When?"

Inner elation. "Is tomorrow too soon?"

"That's fine. We're going to the grocery store."

Tears of relief and gratitude.

My parents drove eight hours to our house. I'll never forget going out to greet them. The garage door went up, and there they were. This day had been a long time coming, and I immediately ran to them. I met Dad first. Instinctively, I hugged him, and he held me as I cried, drawing me tighter as I shook with sobs. Wordlessly, I reached for my mom as we wept together, her face wet with tears.

> ## And call on me in the day of trouble; I will deliver you, and you will honor me.
>
> —PSALM 50:15 (NIV)

Mom and Dad stayed with us for several weeks. They followed my directions in caring for the girls and quickly overcame their fear of doing something wrong. They not only took care of the kids when I spent long days in the hospital with Brad, but also brought the kids to the hospital to see their daddy.

My dad was there when volunteers set up the wheelchair ramps outside. He was also there the night we changed our den into a hospital room for Brad. I couldn't face this decision and sat comatose, staring. But Dad got the dolly and moved furniture.

"Where do you want this?" he asked, and I pointed.

"Where do you want this?" he asked again, indicating another piece of equipment. Again, all I could do was point.

GOD'S GIFT OF HEARING
— By Lawrence W. Wilson —

COMATOSE PATIENTS LACK motor control and cannot speak. Their eyes are usually closed. Yet they can retain the ability to hear. EEG testing has proven that the brain of a comatose patient can react to sound. Caregivers recommend that family members talk to loved ones who are unconscious, announcing their presence and chatting about their activities. This is not unlike the function of the Holy Spirit, who speaks to the unconscious mind. Even those who do not appear to respond may be reacting to the voice of God at a spiritual level (see Romans 8:16).

I couldn't move or speak as my brain struggled to process Brad's recovery process. Dad put up the shower curtain I purchased to add privacy to the room, and he removed a door so Brad could wheel into the kitchen.

After Brad settled in at home, we hit a groove with his care. When we were ready to tackle it on our own, my parents returned home. I have never been so grateful for God's provision.

As Brad's feet healed, God healed our hearts and the relationships between my parents, my husband, and me. His injuries and extended recovery had opened the door. God graciously used brokenness and injury to bring incredible healing to my husband's feet and our family's hearts.

Ordinary Man, Extraordinary Vision

By Patricia McClurg

He sat in his cramped basement office, head in his hands, shoulders hunched. The harsh glare of fluorescent light fought the dark energy filling the space. The desk was a large wooden cast-off we'd found abandoned in the last house we'd owned. Folders were scattered across the surface. I sat beside my husband, Lynn, in a folding chair we kept for moments when private talks needed to happen behind a closed door. He took a deep breath and sighed with resignation.

"I can't keep doing this anymore, Patty. I give my word to merchants, and the company keeps adding hidden fees to the bills. My word and my testimony for Christ are constantly jeopardized."

I heard the tension in his voice. "What can you do?" I ask.

"I can call and ask them to remove the fees. When I've done this in the past, they told me I make more money if I leave the fees there. They tell me the fees benefit *both* the rep and the company. Each time, I call and say, 'Not my merchants.' So far, they do what I ask, but they're angry to see the fees. It appears like I changed the deal behind their backs. How long before they change the terms of the deal on me and refuse to adjust the fees for my vendors? I can't keep fighting. It's only getting worse."

I put my hand on his shoulder. I'd seen my husband lose jobs over and over. When we first got married, Lynn was working as a respiratory therapist in a hospital, and he transitioned to managing a medical home-care company. But government regulations and insurance contracts changed, draining profits from home-care oxygen and equipment rentals. As large companies acquired smaller companies, duplicate employees in management were let go. Twice Lynn was ousted in mergers.

> **For we are taking pains to do what is right, not only in the eyes of the Lord but also in the eyes of man.**
>
> —2 CORINTHIANS 8:21 (NIV)

For the next five years, Lynn focused on building a portfolio of merchants in credit card processing. In faith, he left the house every day and asked God, "Where do I go today? Who do I talk to today?" He drove all over the state cultivating new clients, and God faithfully provided. Over and over again, I'd seen him reinvent himself in the workforce.

But I'd never seen him so beaten down, defeated, and weary as he hunched over his desk.

Lord, give me wisdom to help him. I don't know what to say.

"If you could do anything in the world, what would you choose?" If we were going to start all over again, we might as well go for it.

"Sell a God-honoring product that changed people's lives," Lynn responded quickly.

Piece of cake. God-honoring product that changes lives. On it. God?

Immediately, I recalled having tea with a friend from church. She was lamenting her cash flow challenges after her husband invested large sums of money creating a product they couldn't sell. I didn't believe in coincidence, so I told Lynn about it.

"Jeannie told me Ron invested his money in a product he can't sell. Maybe you should talk to him and see what it is."

Intrigued, Lynn went to see Ron, returned, and told me Ron had created a God-honoring product that changed lives— an Internet accountability program that would help men and women break free from bondage. I saw new light in Lynn's eyes. He'd found more than a product—he'd found a vision and a mission.

Driven by a desire to know if this connection was from God, my husband and I secluded ourselves in a hotel away from our children for a weekend so we could focus on seeking God's wisdom. Soon after arriving, we settled across from each other at a little brown table, and I pulled out my notepad and pen. Lynn decided to begin by describing the product and what it did. However, because it was a digital service and not a tangible, hands-on product, wording the description proved difficult. His frustration became evident as his voice shifted from excitement to doubt, and his expression moved from alight with possibilities to dark with doubt.

Lynn had never sold a digital product before, and he struggled to know how to sell such an item. Ron's partner was a teenage tech wizard, and their two years of investment in their product had netted them just 174 customers. The first time Lynn met with Ron, he learned that Ron had recently attempted to give his business away and could find no takers.

Lynn and I bantered back and forth, verbally exploring possibilities. We made list after list and weighed this option against that option from a variety of perspectives. What was the upside? What was the downside? Who might buy this product? How and where would Lynn and I find these customers? And what was the worst that could happen? Hadn't we experienced worst-case scenarios before?

Then, taking my hands across the table, Lynn got down to the bottom line.

"I can't take Ron's money when I don't know if I can sell this thing. The pressure would be distracting and set me up to fail. Pressure doesn't work for me in sales. God's heart is for service, and I see myself as a servant. Do you think my servant approach to selling will work with this product? I don't feel like I can walk away from something that can so powerfully change lives. God seems to have put this opportunity in front of me. I must hear from Him about what to do because I can only do this if He is in it."

Lynn and I went to separate spaces in our room to pray, asking for wisdom and peace from God about what to do. Then we went to bed.

In the morning, we sat at the table again and talked about what we'd heard from God. Amazingly, He'd given both of us peace to take a risk unlike any we'd ever taken before. I left the hotel proud of a husband who was willing to risk so much on God's faithfulness.

Lynn called Ron and told him, "I will sell your product on one condition. You can't pay me. If I make it successful, I want an equal share in the company."

At the time, we didn't know that Ron and his wife, Jeannie, had been persistently praying for a person to help them sell their product. They'd even made a list of specific character and professional qualities they wanted in a partner: a person with successful sales experience, strong work ethic, and strong personal integrity; a self-starter; and a mature Christian with a foundation in God's Word. They had only one condition on their list—that the person be willing to "work for free." The last of their cash flow had been spent on a salesman who'd been unable to produce results.

> **Pray for us. We are sure that we have a clear conscience and desire to live honorably in every way.**
>
> **—HEBREWS 13:18 (NIV)**

Based upon his agreement with Ron, Lynn let his credit card business go dormant, sold his credit card portfolio, and was not paid by Ron's business for two and a half years. Lynn, a former respiratory therapist who was self-taught in sales, an ordinary guy from a village in mid-Michigan working out of his basement, grew sales for Covenant Eyes Inc. from 174 customers to 600 customers in six months and 3,000 customers in one year. Today, Covenant Eyes is a $30-million-a-year employee-owned company, with sales in countries all over the world. It offers a God-honoring product that changes people's lives because one man—my husband—was willing to believe in and trust God for extraordinary results.

Hovering at the Threshold

By Sue Schuerman

For several weeks I felt like someone was watching me as I walked down the hall at the retirement community where I worked. When I looked around, everything seemed normal—residents solving a puzzle, nurses answering call lights, maintenance people repairing an air conditioner. But this eerie feeling continued to trail me down the hallway.

Then one day, a nurse's aide stopped in front of me, blocking my path. She looked at me with eyes that knew more than I understood.

"Were you born September 26?" She stood closer than I wished.

"Yes." I nodded.

She threw her arms around me in an I'm-never-going-to-let-you-go embrace, then stood back, cupping my cheeks in her palms. "I knew it. You have the family eyes, dark hair, slight build."

Is she crying? Who is this woman?

"Your birthday is the same as mine. I'll never forget the day you were born."

I drew back and tried to recall the voice, the face, anything that would help me place this person who obviously knew me. She seemed oblivious to my hesitation, to my not knowing. And we were starting to collect an audience.

She continued. "Thick, dark eyebrows, dark-brown eyes. Oh, Susie, we lost track of you and now here you are standing right in front of me. I can't believe my prayers have been answered!"

"Let's visit in my office," I suggested, as I directed her toward the door.

Later that evening I related this uncanny experience to my husband. "You won't believe what happened to me today. I'm not even sure I can explain it. This woman, a nurse's aide, accosted me in the hallway at work. Well, she didn't really accost me, she just startled me, maybe even turned my life upside down." I gazed out the window, praying for answers in the starlit heavens.

"Well, just start at the beginning," my husband urged.

"Her name is Dona. She's my aunt—my birth mother's sister." I threw my hands in the air. "She appeared out of the blue, and now she wants me to meet the woman who gave me life!"

Honour thy father and thy mother: that thy days may be long upon the land which the LORD thy God giveth thee.

—EXODUS 20:12 (KJV)

I shouldn't have been surprised. When I was fourteen years old, I learned that I had two mothers—one who raised me and one who brought me into the world. At that time, my interests were focused on my friends and school. I loved my family and didn't see the need to add anyone else to the mix. Years passed and I became immersed in raising a family and building my career. It never occurred to me to connect with my birth mother.

And now Aunt Dona was suggesting I contact her sister. We lived more than eleven hundred miles apart, a sixteen-hour drive or a two-and-a-half-hour flight. Dona had handed me a slip of paper with a phone number and address.

Would this woman who gave me life even *want* to talk to me? She hadn't made contact for thirty-six years. Did I want to involve another mother in my life? It felt like a betrayal of the mother who'd raised me to meet "another mother." I waffled with these thoughts and questions for weeks. How would I address her? "Mom" or "mother" seemed too intimate. I settled on her nickname, Tiny.

I'd spent my adult life creating stability and structure, and now those things were unexpectedly being threatened. I hovered at this threshold.

In the meantime, another aunt started writing to me. Aunt Bette lived in Dallas. She was the older sister of Dona and Tiny. At this time, email was a foreign concept, so we enjoyed old-fashioned handwritten notes. I treasured her warm, friendly letters and felt a kinship grow through our writings. She sent me hand-painted cards, and I sent her cards decorated with my calligraphy. She signed her letters, "I love you. May God bless you." Still, I hesitated to reach out to Tiny. Surely her sisters must have told her they found me. Why hadn't she reached out to me?

During this same time, I was offered a serendipitous opportunity to travel to Dallas for a work conference. I couldn't allow this divine opportunity to wither. Nudged by an unseen Presence, I wrote to Aunt Bette to see if I could meet her for lunch while I was at the conference. Her response warmed my heart. Not only did she agree to drive to the conference center, but she also invited me to stay overnight at her house.

Buoyed by this invitation, I also wrote to Tiny, asking if she could meet us in Dallas. I told her I would love to spend time with her and Aunt Bette.

Then I crossed my fingers.

I prayed.

I paced the floor.

Several weeks later, Tiny's reply arrived in the mail. Too excited, too nervous to open the envelope, I asked my husband to read me her response. Because it was a five-hour drive from her home near San Antonio, Tiny declined.

I pressed my hand to my heart and released a deep sigh. All in God's timing, I reminded myself.

Disappointed yet relieved, I was determined to know this woman better—at a distance. Over the next year, we exchanged letters and photographs. Tiny was a gifted gardener, crafter, seamstress, and writer. Also, an avid reader and lifelong learner.

"Wow," I said to my husband. "We share so many interests. I wonder if we'll ever meet." Words from Ecclesiastes echoed in my mind: There is a season, a time for every activity under heaven.

A few days after I expressed that thought, I rushed home from work, breathless with great news to tell my husband. "This is amazing. Hold on to your hat. My work conference is in San Antonio this year."

He wrinkled his forehead and raised his eyebrows, "And that means…"

"That's thirty minutes from where Tiny lives. And it's amazing because the conference is never held in the same state two years in a row. It's a miracle! It is the time. It is the season." Goose bumps tickled my skin.

A few months later, a battered yellow cab dropped me off on a dusty Texas street lined with antique shops, taverns, and a small café, just a few miles south of San Antonio. I found myself walking toward a woman with silky gray hair. She wore navy slacks and a homemade vest with appliquéd flowers in yellow and red. They matched the bouquet I extended toward her.

Another coincidence?

Each step I took felt like I was trudging through a mire. I didn't know if I should hug her, wait for her to hug me first, or skip the hug altogether. But Tiny's warm smile melted the awkward moment. Her embrace didn't equal the forever hug of Aunt Dona. It was more like a friend's joyful greeting. Both of us were flushed bright pink. At last I was in the arms of my birth mother. We stepped apart and grinned. It was like looking at a reflection of myself in a pool of water.

> **Thy father and thy mother shall be glad, and she that bare thee shall rejoice.**
>
> **—PROVERBS 23:25 (KJV)**

We entered the simple mom-and-pop café Tiny had suggested. The plastic red-and-white-checked tablecloths sharply contrasted the white linen gracing the tables at the four-star hotel I'd just left. At first I thought the café was an odd place to meet a daughter for the first time, but I soon learned it fit Tiny's simple, no-fuss lifestyle.

Tiny spread photos on the table. She lived alone in a mobile home in the country, surrounded by trees, gardens, and lots of wildlife. Our lunch sat untouched as our conversation brought us together and our water glasses were filled again and again.

GOD'S GIFT OF TOUCH
— By Tez Brooks —

THERE ARE OTHER experiences for touch beyond physical. At times it's emotional, even spiritual. Hearts are touched by kindness, lives touched by someone's intervention, or souls touched by God's love. Hebrews 4:15 reveals how man's troubles touch the Lord's heart. He understands. He was here experiencing life on earth for himself. Jesus touched blind eyes, deaf ears, speechless tongues, even those with leprosy who were "untouchable" and healed them all. But this went beyond the physical to their emotional and spiritual needs. Christ is the same today. Individuals can come to him and find sympathy and grace for comfort and salvation.

Finally, she gingerly placed a black-and-white photo of a baby on the tablecloth.

"This is you at three days old."

I was wrapped in a blanket, snuggled next to a young woman who beheld her baby with adoration that rivaled Mother Mary and the Christ Child. Tiny looked at me with gentle eyes.

"You know, I've always loved you."

My hands formed a steeple as I pressed them to my lips. At that moment we crossed the threshold together—forever bound by divine love.

Twenty Years a-Prayin'

By Donna Schlachter

"Hell will freeze over before I apologize to him. And he will never meet my children."

My sister Cathy's words hung heavy through the telephone between us. She was always the strong-willed child, the youngest of three girls, and the one best characterized as quick to anger and slow to forgive.

So much like the man she referred to. Our father.

Whom she'd not spoken to in twenty years.

During that time, much had changed. His second wife passed away, and now he called another the love of his life. He'd gone from a youngish man of sixty to one rapidly approaching his eighth decade. My sister now had two children in junior high who'd never met their maternal grandfather.

What would create such a chasm between a father and his youngest daughter, so deep and wide he'd written her out of his will and never even mentioned her name? When asked how many children he had, he said four instead of the actual five.

And she—what did she say about him? Did she curse his name? Wish she'd been born into a different family? Did she look in the mirror and see him staring back at her in the shape of her nose, the tilt of her chin, the set of her mouth?

And what would it take to mend the wounds of hurtful words and miscommunication?

As it turned out, it took twenty years of prayer by my younger sister and me. Along with God's unfailing presence, directing not only their lives, but also the lives of His people around them.

I identify the origin of this discord between my sister and father as a serious car accident my sister experienced twenty years before our phone conversation. For weeks, her condition hovered between critical and hopeless. My father, who then served on a regional hospital board, flew to be with her, hoping to use his connections to ensure his little girl received the best health care.

But he forgot one thing: She had a husband, who was the one to determine what happened with my sister.

These two men, who never liked the other and trusted each other even less, clashed in a hospital room, one on either side of my sister, who lay in a coma.

> **Be kind to one another, tenderhearted, forgiving one another, as God in Christ forgave you.**
>
> —EPHESIANS 4:32 (ESV)

"Michael, you forget one thing. I'm her husband. I'm the one who makes the choices about her care."

My father gripped the bed railing. Machines beeped, raising strange lightning-jagged lines that reported heart rate—normal—and brain function—low. "But I want her to get the best care. I've already put a call in—"

"And you're not listening."

"I am. I can have her transported—"

"No."

My dad stared at him. Thomas, his arms folded across his chest and his shoulders rigid, faced him down. Immovable opposing immovable. "Don't you want the best for her?"

"She's getting it. This is a Level One trauma center."

"But—"

"No."

A doctor entered the room and nod- ded to each. "Mr. Miller. Mr. Wells." My father backed away and walked down the hall, alone. Leaving his daughter in her husband's hands.

Six months passed as my sister slowly recovered. A traumatic brain injury left her with fractured memories of her life before the accident. My brother-in-law undertook filling in the blanks for her, often tainted with his own version of events. Cathy gave me examples later in her recovery.

My sister had recalled feelings of ambivalence toward Peter, the man she'd divorced several years earlier. "You know, Cathy, that could mean you were abused," Thomas said, as he sat beside her in the rehab center one day. "I've heard that can mess up your life so you don't want intimacy."

"I don't remember being abused. You mean when I was a kid?"

"Exactly. See, your mind tries to bury those memories. And when they surface, your psyche wants to make sense of them. I'm sure that's what happened to you."

"But who would do that to me?" Cathy implored.

"Well, think back. Did any men in your family pay special attention to you? Touch you? Things like that?"

The discussion continued, until, while she had no direct recall of any sexual abuse, Thomas had convinced Cathy she was a victim.

She'd called me the next day. "I was sexually abused as a child."

"I doubt it."

"Well, I was."

I didn't want to hear this. I wasn't calling her a liar, but I sincerely doubted what she was saying. "So, how did you figure this out?"

"Thomas helped me remember."

My antennae perked up. I knew of the breach between my brother-in-law and my father, of course. I'd spoken with them, suggesting they both had Cathy's best interests at heart. Surely, they could come to an agreement.

Neither listened.

"Really? How?" I pressed.

"Well, we were talking about Peter, and Thomas said maybe I didn't want intimacy with him because of some repressed memories."

Since when had her husband become such an expert on childhood sexual abuse? "You told me when you divorced Peter that you'd never loved him in that way. You felt more like his sister and he your brother."

"But I remember that I was sexually abused."

"Do you really recall the situation and the person?"

"Well, I know who it must have been."

I wouldn't allow incorrect memories to destroy them and the rest of my family. "Unless you have an actual memory not suggested by Thomas, I don't want to hear about it."

And so, we never talked about it again. But the relationship between my sister and our father had fractured. Irretrievably, it seemed. Neither one mentioned the other in conversations.

One thing I determined was not to treat either my dad or my sister as being dead when I talked with the other. I made certain to include information about the other I had in conversations with them, just as I would if they were still communicating. Silence usually met my words, but I didn't care.

Well, I did care. So much that I prayed constantly for both to realize Jesus's love for them, their need for Him, and their need to forgive.

The years passed slowly. One. Two. Five. Ten. Nothing changed. I wondered if God would ever answer.

Fast-forward another ten years. The same brother-in-law I never connected with called and asked me to talk to his wife, my sister, about her need to reconcile with her father. He'd been estranged for years from his mother and had recently reached out to her. He wanted the same for his wife.

> **For if you forgive others their trespasses, your heavenly Father will also forgive you.**
>
> **—MATTHEW 6:14 (ESV)**

After he put her on the phone, my sister and I had a long conversation.

"Cathy, you and Dad both messed up. But somebody needs to be the adult and call. Admit your mistake. Apologize. Ask to start over."

"Well, it won't be me making that call."

I sighed. "One of these days, one of you will be dead, and it will be too late. And the other will have to live the rest of your life knowing that you can't fix it."

That's when my sister told me hell would freeze over.

We said our goodbyes and hung up, but the ache in my heart remained.

My husband and I prayed about the situation, and almost twenty-four hours later, Cathy called and asked for Dad's phone number. I wasn't sure whether I wanted to subject him to her anger.

"What will you say to him?"

"That we both messed up. We both made mistakes. That we need to start new and move forward."

I chuckled inside because she said it like it was coming from her heart.

Well, they moved forward with a meeting a few months later, and Dad met two grandchildren he'd only ever heard about from me or my other sister. In July of that year, Cathy traveled to celebrate Dad's eightieth birthday and our family reunion. In early December, Dad received Jesus as his Savior. Three weeks later he passed away, over twenty years after my younger sister and I began praying for him.

It's the Small Things

By Patricia McClurg

As I was sitting on the floor of the Humane Society break room, a tiny, white, partially bald bag of skin and bones flitted from my mom to me, to the volunteer, and back to each of us, in random order. One dark, orbed eye darted frantically as the dog attempted to find a safe place. The other eye, atrophied and gray, was of no support in this quest.

"This is Phoebe," the lanky young man said from across the room. "She's shy around strangers, and she's been rescued twice. Her right side was badly injured at one time. She's eleven and a half years old and underweight at just five pounds thirteen ounces. We guess she's a combination of toy poodle and long-haired Chihuahua."

My eyes followed the dog in her never-ending circle as the volunteer continued. "You can probably see that Phoebe didn't receive medical attention."

I smiled. Her ears were too big for her tiny head, and her tail resembled a broken fan. She reminded me of a pitiful character I once saw in a musical, and my heart wrapped around this dog.

Earlier that day, my mom, with a heart that beats for rescue dogs needing homes, had seen a picture of Phoebe in a local newspaper ad for the Humane Society. She'd handed me the paper and said, "*This dog* is for you. *You* need this dog."

I'd mentally rolled my eyes and said, "We aren't looking for a dog. We have one." But then I looked at the picture—frightened, dark eyes peeking out from a tiny, white, partly fuzzy head.

I'd swallowed, then quickly reached for my keys and told Mom I'd pick her up on the way to the shelter.

Now, looking at the shuddering creature that stared at me from behind the volunteer's chair, my heart was conflicted. She would need medical care if we adopted her. Her life had been rough, but she appeared to be a curious and joyful little thing.

"Really, this dog is meant for you. She *needs* you." My mom again.

I asked a few more questions, but if I was really considering adoption, I knew what I must do. I stepped

Trust in the LORD with all your heart and lean not on your own understanding; in all your ways submit to him, and he will make your paths straight.

—PROVERBS 3:5–6 (NIV)

into the hall, reached for my phone, and called my husband. Precious man that he is, he left me with a reassuring admonition: "I trust you to do the right thing."

Well, I concluded, *obviously, the "right thing" is to adopt her. How many chances will a twice-rejected senior dog with medical issues get?*

The decision was mine, and I couldn't ignore her now because God had obviously placed Phoebe in my path.

Returning the next day to complete paperwork, I adopted Phoebe, loaded the car, and drove three long hours home.

Phoebe began the journey trembling and eventually fell asleep in the dog bed for the entire trip. I mused as I drove.

Her whole life was changing. She had no idea what lay at the other end of this trip, yet she slept peacefully. In this "now" moment, she was safe and comfortable. The anxiety that clung to her when we began this journey had slipped away. *Father, You tell me in Your Word not to be anxious. My anxiety adds nothing to the length of my days. Tomorrow will take care of itself. Each day has enough trouble of its own. Yet I can't seem to rest like Phoebe and trust You like she trusts me. It is hard, Father.*

I took a deep breath. My fingers relaxed their grip around the steering wheel. Trust is a choice.

But once we arrived home, my choice to love Phoebe was tested. Night after night, she lay shuddering in her crate, crying, barking what I imagine are the questions, "Why am I alone? Is someone there?"

For the next year and a half, our nighttime peace remained shattered. Every night with incremental intention, we altered Phoebe's bedtime routine and attained micro successes, rising multiple times a night to correct her.

Then one night before bedtime, Phoebe cowered outside her crate across the room in our bedroom and stared at us with her one dark eye, silently begging us not to put her inside.

My husband, Lynn, and I sat up in bed and spoke to her to calm her, and I flipped on my bedside light. As I watched her trembling body and slipped out of bed to comfort her, a revelation hit me.

"Lynn, I think we've been doing this wrong." I crouched down and stroked Phoebe's body. "We've depended on the crate to comfort her, like the dog books tell us. But I think she's telling me that *I'm* her source of comfort." I heard the voice of the Holy Spirit nudge me, saying, "I am your Comforter."

I picked up Phoebe and carried her to the living room, where I retrieved the dog bed that sat near my chair. I brought it back to the bedroom, placed her in it, and attached her leash to my nightstand.

"I think you've figured out something life-changing for Phoebe and for us, Patty," Lynn observed, as Phoebe immediately curled up in her bed. She slept peacefully through that night and every night since. Her presence beside me in the dark reminds me that I can *choose* to trust God in dark times and rest in the peace of His presence. Just like my broken dog, I, too, tremble for fear of things that have hurt me.

I took this thought with me one morning as I settled at the kitchen table for a cup of tea before the rest of the family stirred. The house was quiet, and my gaze settled on Phoebe, who had followed me and was searching for the dog bed near my feet. Out of love for our Phoebe, we kept a dog bed for her comfort near my favorite sitting spot in every room.

She was now almost completely blind, cataracts slowly smoldering her sight in her one good eye. Her sense of smell and hearing had also dimmed with age. Wherever I went, she searched for me, her ears at high alert, her head turning from side to side and her little feet high-stepping with focused intention. If I stood in one place, Phoebe's diligent search often passed me by, sometimes within twelve inches.

Lynn appeared in the doorway of the bedroom, still struggling to wake up.

"She doesn't see you, Patty. You're sitting too still."

I called out to Phoebe and wiggled my "come-here" fingers close to her face. She cautiously sniffed my hand, then joyously drew close, like she had found a long-lost love. No matter her pain or physical losses, as long as Phoebe was with me, she was content.

God? Why does it take me so long to learn that all I need is You, when my dog can find contentment in a flawed human like me?

Lynn came to sit near me in his own chair. The past few years had drained us. I watched my husband battle Covid-19 and an intense migraine for days that made me fear he would have a stroke. Exhausted and with diminished lung capacity after my own Covid fight, I nursed him, took him to the ER, and remained at his bedside. Then we were left with more grief when our daughter's surgery to provide relief for a painful medical condition didn't produce our hoped-for results. During those dark days, we did not see God's fingers drawing us to Him.

> Let the morning bring me word of your unfailing love, for I have put my trust in you. Show me the way I should go, for to you I entrust my life.
>
> —PSALM 143:8 (NIV)

Since adopting Phoebe four years ago, she's grown to weigh seven pounds, developed abundant curly white hair, and has a tail like small ostrich feathers. She's been an instrument in God's hand to open my eyes and revive my heart. When I wasn't expecting it, God impacted my life through Phoebe, a tiny creature in need of care.

As it turns out, Mom was right. I needed this dog, and she needed me. Our lives are better together. Phoebe has taught me that small, ordinary, insignificant things like our traumatized and rejected pooch, when in the Maker's hands, can heal hearts, open eyes, and change lives like mine.

GOD'S GIFT OF TOUCH
— By Tez Brooks —

MANATEES CAN TOUCH from a distance, meaning they can feel things without touching them. A manatee's body is covered with thousands of whiskers, allowing them to sense things through pressure. They notice changes in their surroundings like currents and tides. But the most awesome thing about this gift is the ability to stroke, handle, and measure objects from afar. Their hairs determine when something dangerous is approaching, if food is floating toward them, or if a submerged tree trunk is blocking their route. This makes them the animal with the strongest sense of touch.

We *all* have angels guiding, guarding us…. we see them only briefly, like footprints before the tide comes in and washes clean the sand. Angels everywhere. What will bring their help? Asking. Giving thanks.

—Sophy Burnham, writer

CHAPTER 6

Angels on Earth

I Met a Guardian Angel

By Mindy Baker

In college I spent a semester living as a foreign exchange student in Seville, Spain. Seville is a picturesque city along the Guadalquivir River in southern Spain where the smell of oranges is always in the air. It boasts a blend of Moorish, Gothic, and Renaissance architecture and is a place where you can experience flamenco shows, bullfights, and relaxing horse-drawn carriage rides. I used to love to wander the winding, narrow corridors of the Jewish quarter, and I couldn't get enough of browsing the ceramic and tile shops and sampling the famous Spanish cuisine like paella, gazpacho, and tapas.

The family I stayed with gave me a key to their high-rise apartment on Calle Felipe II in the El Porvenir neighborhood, and they offered me only one guideline: "Don't walk at night alone through the nearby Parque de Maria Luisa." Seemed simple enough. Their advice made sense, and I followed it—for a while.

But as a young college student with not a lot of extra money, my go-to mode of transportation was my feet. I walked everywhere. And as time went on during my stay in Seville, I became more and more acclimated to the city. The more comfortable I became with my surroundings, the more my attitude toward the Parque de Maria Luisa shifted. Instead of seeing it as a possible danger, it became a huge inconvenience. Walking around it took forever, and it was much shorter to simply cut through it. I easily rationalized this behavior by telling myself that I wasn't purposefully and intentionally spending long periods of time strolling through the park—I was simply taking a tiny shortcut.

One night, while ignoring the advice of my host family and cutting through the park, I noticed a group of young men off in the distance. Their voices and raucous laughter echoed into the night, but I couldn't make out what they were saying. They were speaking in Spanish, and although I was studying the language, I wasn't fluent. They were playing loud music, and there was the smell of smoke wafting in my direction. My gut instinct was to turn and run. It was obvious to me that they were not a wholesome group of young gentlemen. And I was alone.

> **For he will command his angels concerning you to guard you in all your ways.**
>
> —PSALM 91:11 (NIV)

With heart pounding, I weighed my options. If I turned around to go back to the entrance of the park and walked around it, I would arrive late to my destination. If I stayed on this shorter course and walked by the group, I would arrive on time. Foolishly, I kept going, thinking to myself that they were probably busy doing their own thing and wouldn't notice me.

As I neared the group of young men, a stranger appeared and started walking with me. I couldn't discern exactly from which direction he came, but he appeared to be going the same way I was. I remember that he was fairly tall and rather average-looking, with shoulder-length, wavy brown hair, and he spoke to me in English. I don't recall how our conversation started, but I do remember chatting comfortably about everyday information like where I attended classes during the day, where I was from, and where I was going that evening. Nothing too deep.

The way of fools seems right to them, but the wise listen to advice.

—PROVERBS 12:15 (NIV)

As we walked by the group of young men, they whistled and called out comments, but this stranger and I passed by without incident. We kept walking and talking together until finally he said he needed to turn around. He didn't say why. I do remember his last words as we parted: "You really shouldn't walk alone in the park." I turned away to keep walking toward my destination and thought about what he said. When I glanced back to look at him again, he was gone. Vanished. Almost as if he had never been there in the first place.

Then the whole thing hit me all at once, and I started shaking. Had I dreamed all of that? My mind raced as I recalled the entire incident in slow motion. It felt so normal, walking and talking with this stranger. And in the moment, nothing seemed out of the ordinary.

As the years have passed, I have never been able to shake the thought that God sent an angel that night to protect me from my own foolishness. I will never know for certain this side of heaven, but I do believe that stranger was a guardian angel.

GOD'S GIFT OF HEARING
— By Eryn Lynum —

THE WORLD FALLS quiet beneath a blanket of snow. Snowfall swallows and absorbs surrounding noise, similar to acoustic sound dampeners in a music room. Psalm 131:2 (NIV) says, "I have calmed and quieted myself." At times, when the volume of circumstances rises to a deafening level, God steps in like a fresh snowfall to quiet the souls of His children so that they may hear His voice above all other noise. Absorbing the clatter, He brings calm, peace, and perspective.

The Blessing of a Flat Tire

By Rhoda Blecker

Before he went out of town, the rabbi asked me to lead Torah study on Saturday morning. I'd done it before, but each time he asked, I felt a little apprehensive. Shabbat morning Torah study is an important practice for many members of our congregation, and I wanted to do a good job for the people who faithfully showed up at the synagogue to participate. We believe that God speaks to us through the text of the first five books (Genesis, Exodus, Leviticus, Numbers, and Deuteronomy); being a guide to God's messages meant much preparation in advance.

On Friday I read through the portion for the week, studied some rabbinic interpretations written by scholars in the past several thousand years, pulled out information that spoke to me, chose the specific verses for study, and photocopied materials to hand out to the attendees. I carefully put the material next to my purse, along with the synagogue keys and the directions for turning off the alarm code. I double-checked it all before I went to bed and set my alarm for two hours before the session was to start. I thought I was entirely ready. I slept well, confident I could at least get the discussion going; after that, I thought it would likely take off by itself.

I was awake before the alarm went off Saturday morning. I lived only ten minutes from the synagogue and was sure if I left a half hour before study was to begin, I would be able to unlock the building and have the social hall set up in plenty of time before anyone else arrived. My morning prayer that day was, "I think I've got it covered, God, and I'll try to do a good job."

There is a saying: "If you want to hear God laugh, just tell God your plans." I drove out my driveway to the side street, then made the left turn that took me onto one of the main roads. At that point, my car began making *pfump, pfump* noises and became much harder to drive. I pulled as far to the right as I could, moved the gearshift to Park, turned on the hazard lights, and got out to see what was going on.

My right front tire was flat. So flat, in fact, that the hubcap seemed to be touching the road surface. I stared at it stupidly for a few moments before I started trying to decide what to do next. All I could think was, "I *have* to get to the synagogue." People would be showing up and standing around the locked door. If I couldn't get there, they wouldn't be able to get in to study. It was my responsibility. And just as I didn't want to disappoint them, I didn't want to disappoint the rabbi.

Will He not cause all my success?

—2 SAMUEL 23:5 (TANAKH)

I ran through a short list of possibilities: (a) I belonged to the auto club, but if I called them, they were unlikely to get to me before study was supposed to start; I probably wouldn't arrive at the synagogue until after the other potential participants had given up and gone home. So that wouldn't work. (b) Based on past performance, if I tried to change the tire myself, I was not going to get to the synagogue by Sunday! So that was not a viable alternative either.

That left (c), which gave me my best chance of making it. I would drive on the flat tire and destroy it, but I might get there on time. Once I was back in the car, I realized I could not go faster than about fifteen miles per hour. At that speed, I thought I might just arrive when I needed to, or at least not more than a couple of minutes late. I left my hazard lights on and began a slow crawl, taking my usual route through town. Luckily, I could turn off the main road very soon, and there was little traffic on the side streets I drove every Shabbat on my way to Torah study. I was regretting I hadn't left home earlier, but then who knew this was going to happen?

My normal journey to the synagogue took me past the red brick building that housed the Bellingham Food Bank, which was closed on Saturdays. In all the months I had been traveling past it every week, I had never seen anyone standing outside. As my car limped toward the building that day, however, I was surprised to see three people in the parking lot: a woman and two men. They looked up as the car approached, perhaps alerted by the ongoing *pfump*ing sounds. The three of them immediately started in my direction, waving and pointing at the tire, almost as if they thought I didn't know it was flat.

I debated driving past—there was very little time left before I had to be at the synagogue, and it was still about five minutes away at my speed—but I really didn't want to be rude. I pulled over and rolled the passenger side window down. "I have to teach a class at nine thirty," I began.

The woman interrupted me. "Do you have a spare tire?" she asked.

"Yes," I said, "but—"

She overrode my objection. "Pop your trunk," she ordered.

One of the men was already standing behind my car, reinforcing her command with an "open it!" gesture.

They were both so intense that I unthinkingly pulled the trunk release, then turned off the engine and got out of the car. The second man came over to me as his friend pulled out my emergency spare, rolled it to the woman, and grabbed my jack.

The man next to me was grinning broadly. "What class are you teaching?" he asked. I looked at him, then at my watch.

"I teach Bible study," I said, so as not to have to explain what the Torah was, in case he didn't know. "And I have to be there in about four minutes."

Still with a grin on his face, he asked, "Do you know who Dan Gurney is?"

The name was vaguely familiar, so I said, "I think I've heard of him before, but—" I gave him an "I can't place him" wave with both hands.

"He was a champion NASCAR and Formula One driver," the man said. "We were on his pit crew."

I looked over at the car and realized that the other two people already had my tire changed, and the woman was tightening the lugs on the wheel, lamenting that she had to use a mechanical torque wrench instead of a pneumatic one. They tossed the flat tire and the jack into the trunk and slammed it shut. The entire operation had taken less than two minutes.

I fumbled in my purse for money to offer them, but they refused, and the man who'd told me about their racing-spangled past said, "Go teach your class. You're needed." They did make me promise to go directly to a tire place and get new tires as soon as the class was over.

Needless to say, I arrived at the synagogue exactly on time, and I obediently went to the tire store after that. Only then, waiting for my new tires to be installed, did I sit still long enough to realize that I hadn't really prayed, or even thought about God during the whole crisis. But God had sent me exactly the right people so that everything would turn out OK.

> **God is our refuge and strength, a very present help in trouble.**
>
> —PSALMS 46:2 (TANAKH)

Every Saturday for the next two years, until our congregation moved into a new building four miles away, I drove past the food bank on my way to Torah study, hoping to see "my" pit crew again, but there was never anyone outside the building.

Slowly it dawned on me that they had so enjoyed helping me and being a pit crew again, God had not only provided them to me, but had also provided me to them.

The Day an Angel Saved My Son

By Kristen West

I only wish I could've seen what actually happened with my own eyes.

I was a young mother at the time. My days were spent chasing my two small children around while helping keep the books and schedule appointments for my husband's heating and air-conditioning business.

We lived in a house that sat on top of a rugged, West Virginia hill overlooking the captivating Ohio River. The concrete driveway up to our home was steep, winding, and nearly a quarter mile long.

It was a beautiful summer day, and my children had gone outside to play in the yard. I stayed inside to catch up on laundry, dishes, and other household chores. I could hear their giggles and voices along with the periodic yips of our new puppy, Patches, as he tried to join in.

While I was elbow-deep in folding a load of towels, my four-year-old daughter came running through the door, needing to use the bathroom. As she sprinted through, she announced that she'd left Philip and Patches in the front yard.

Aware that my son, nearly eighteen months old, was alone outside with Patches didn't faze me at all. Philip couldn't walk very fast yet and wouldn't go very far in the space of time it would take his older sister to use the bathroom.

Poor assumption.

I stopped folding as I realized I wasn't hearing giggles or barking anymore. Just silence. I went to the door and glanced in the yard. Nothing. Neither my son nor our puppy was visible. Thinking there was a possibility they headed to the backyard, I ran to check there. Again, nothing.

I began fervently calling my son's name. "PHILIP!"

Silence.

Now, my heart sank and the adrenaline began to kick in.

My daughter had returned from her bathroom break, and I immediately enlisted her to help me find her brother and the puppy. We both started yelling and looking everywhere—under the porch, under the back deck, in the wooded area next to our property, and over the steep backyard embankment that plummeted into the river.

Nothing.

They were nowhere to be found and neither one was answering as we called.

> ### Ask, and it will be given to you; seek, and you will find.
>
> —MATTHEW 7:7 (NKJV)

The adrenaline surge had morphed into sheer panic as I started to rapidly walk down our long driveway, calling Philip's name at the top of my lungs.

Surely, they didn't come down here, I thought to myself. *They wouldn't have had time.*

Between yells, I would quickly pray, "Oh, God, please show me where he is. Please, Father, PLEASE show me where he is."

I was beginning to get close to the end of our driveway, which fed onto a very busy road. It was a heavily trafficked, two-lane road that cars and eighteen-wheelers used to get from one interstate to another in the area. And this stretch of road wasn't often patrolled by local law enforcement, so many drivers would be reckless and drive well above the speed limit.

Breathless and becoming more desperate by the moment, I finally reached the end of my driveway. What I saw comforted my heart, brought immense relief, and caused complete alarm all at the same time. There on the *other* side of the road, sitting quietly side by side in the grass, were Philip and Patches. My son was smiling. They were both completely peaceful, content, and still. There was no fear, concern, or panic at all.

They were just sitting there. As though they'd been placed there and were being safely kept there.

Almost simultaneously I noted there was no traffic. Not a car or an eighteen-wheeler in sight. I'd *never* seen this road without some sort of traffic on it before (and I never saw it so deserted again after).

It felt like time was standing still. Frozen in the moment. The atmosphere was completely quiet. I didn't even hear any birds. It was surreal—supernatural.

I ran across the road and picked up my little boy, hugging him tightly. As we began our journey back up the driveway, I recalled a dream I had had just a couple nights before. In the dream, my son was crossing a busy street. As he did, a truck was heading toward him, unable to slow down or stop in time to avoid hitting him. Right before the truck was about to strike him, an angel scooped him up and gently sat him down on the other side of the road.

GOD'S GIFT OF SIGHT

— By Eryn Lynum —

WATCHING DAWN'S SKY is like observing a miracle. Moments from now, clouds will be white, but not before proceeding through a symphony of colors. With the sun hanging low on the horizon, its light must travel through more of the atmosphere before reaching the clouds. This longer journey allows blue-colored light waves to scatter, leaving brilliant red, yellow, and orange light waves claiming center stage. Like wavelengths traveling through the atmosphere, the light of God's grace pierces through life's circumstances straight to the souls of His children. The result is a vibrant reflection of His goodness and love.

Although that was all I could remember from the dream, it became abundantly clear to me that my dream had just played out in real life. There was no other explanation for what I had just seen. And while I hadn't witnessed the angel in the act of rescuing my child, I knew—I just *knew*—that is precisely what had happened.

> **For He shall give His angels charge over you, to keep you in all your ways.**
>
> —PSALM 91:11 (NKJV)

I looked at my son and asked him, "Did an angel save you?" I didn't get much of a reply other than a perfect little smile.

God fulfilled His promise of protecting my family that day. He had given an angel charge over my son—to lift him out of harm's way and keep him safe.

That experience opened my heart and my mind to live more expectantly, to be more aware of what was happening around me each and every day (including the things my physical eyes couldn't necessarily see), and to know that God can and does send angels to minister to us—probably more times than we even realize.

No Longer Lost

By Sandy Kirby Quandt

Driving through downtown Houston is something I avoid.
However, if I expected to attend a local one-day writing
conference, that was exactly what I had to do. Armed with
detailed written directions, I set out early that Saturday morning and headed north on Interstate 45. Although the drive to
the conference was stressful, I arrived without getting lost. That
was something I considered a major victory. Upon pulling into
the conference parking lot, I offered up a prayer of thanks. I
also prayed the return trip home would be as uneventful.

After the conference, I looked over my directions one
more time. Again, I prayed for safety on the return drive. My
body tensed, and my grip tightened on the steering wheel
the moment I left the side streets and entered the southbound
feeder lane leading to the interstate.

To my way of thinking, the signage for Houston highways
is not always clear. I missed the entrance onto Interstate 45, and
my reason for not wanting to drive downtown came true. I was
heading in the wrong direction. Instead of heading south on
I-45, I was headed east on an unfamiliar ten-lane major highway full of speeding cars and trucks with no way to exit. There
was no need to look for this highway on the carefully detailed
directions I wrote before leaving for the conference. I knew it
wouldn't be there.

Panic rose. My grip tightened. Concern filled my thoughts. Urgency heightened my prayers.

At the first available exit, I left the highway and pulled into a gas station. The technology existed to pull up a map of Houston on my phone—I just didn't know how to use it. I had never needed to search for a map on my phone before and wasn't sure how. Something so very simple for someone who knows what they are doing became a frustrating and insurmountable technological challenge for me. The harder I tried to pull up the map without success, the more fearful and frustrated I became. It didn't matter how hard I tapped the screen or what I typed into the search bar. I couldn't find what I needed—a way home. Instead, I was lost in an unfamiliar neighborhood.

I put my phone away, took a deep breath, said one more prayer, and walked inside the store with a pen and piece of paper. The clerk behind the counter glared. Still, as far as I saw, he was the only person in the store, and therefore, my only hope for finding a road that would lead me home. My efforts to communicate and explain my problem were met with a shrug and a shake of the clerk's head.

I mumbled my thanks, said another prayer, and turned to leave. Perhaps I could find a different gas station where

> **In my distress I called to the LORD; I cried to my God for help. From his temple he heard my voice; my cry came before him, into his ears.**
>
> **—PSALM 18:6 (NIV)**

someone might help. Those were my thoughts when a man approached. The surprising thing is, I hadn't seen anyone else in the store until he spoke.

"I heard you ask for directions. Where did you say you're needing to go?"

After I told the stranger what happened and where I needed to go, he reached for the pen and paper in my hand. He walked to one of the shelves and began to write. He drew a map and wrote directions next to it. When he was done, he didn't just hand the paper back to me and go on his way. No. This kind gentleman took the time to explain his directions to me.

"When you see the sign for this exit," he said, pointing to the map he drew, "be sure you get all the way over in the left lane. The next exit is the one you need, but getting in the left lane can be tricky. You'll need to work yourself over before you get to your exit. You'll exit on the left."

He looked at me to make sure I understood. I nodded to indicate I did.

As the stranger explained the directions, the fear and frustration I carried with me into the store diminished with each word he spoke. Somehow I knew I could trust this man. I knew if I followed his directions, I would make it home all right. I also knew this stranger—this angel—who could have just as easily ignored my plea for help was an answer to my prayers.

The stranger handed me my pen and notebook. "You sure you got all that?"

"Yes, sir. Get in the left lane ahead of time," I responded.

He smiled.

I wanted to give the man a hug out of pure relief but reached out my hand instead. "Thank you so much. You have no idea how much I appreciate your help."

When he dipped his chin briefly, eyes never leaving mine, I believed maybe he did know.

I pulled out of the gas station and kept the directions the stranger wrote close by. I worked my way into the left lane as soon as I spotted the exit sign, just as he instructed me to do. When I exited onto the road that would take me south instead of carrying me east, I released the breath I wasn't aware I held. I still traveled unfamiliar roads, yet peace replaced the fear that gripped me earlier.

Although I wasn't where I should have been, I was no longer lost. All because God placed a mysterious stranger in a gas station in the middle of a part of town very much unlike my own: a part of town I have never been in before and will probably never be in again. God placed a man who was willing to interrupt his day to draw a map for a stranger in that specific place at that exact moment, so he could overhear my unfruitful conversation with the store clerk and offer his assistance.

> I sought the LORD, and he answered me; he delivered me from all my fears.
>
> —PSALM 34:4 (NIV)

This wasn't the first time God had proved Himself active in my life. But through this chance encounter with a mysterious stranger, God showed me that no matter where I find myself, in familiar surroundings or in a place I have never been before, His constant presence is always with me as He actively provides for my needs. Even when I take the wrong exit and get lost.

How It Worked

By Samuel Pennock

It was a hot summer afternoon. My heart pounded and
my stomach churned as my dad drove me to a rough area
of Philadelphia to attend my first meeting of Narcotics
Anonymous (NA). I was not afraid of the neighborhood or
the dangers there. I had spent a lot of time on streets just like
these. I was terrified of the social situation approaching with no
drugs or alcohol to provide me ease, comfort, and false courage.
I knew the real loser, coward, freak, deviant I believed I was
would be exposed for all to see.

The outpatient services required that I attend NA meetings
as a part of treatment. I did not want to stop using drugs. I was
a social drug user, but my mom insisted I had a problem and
needed treatment. I discovered later that stealing, lying, over-
dosing, prostituting, and using needles to inject drugs is not
considered social use.

I stepped around a junkie passed out by the front door, the
needle still in his arm. *Now*, he *needs help*, I thought. I opened
the glass door and stepped into the old storefront. There was a
desk in the front facing three or four rows of small desk chairs.
To the side was a coffee area; on the walls were two long scrolls
with writing on them and several small picture frames with
slogans inside. I stood tall and strutted in, using all my six-foot-
five-inch height to intimidate, hoping to be left alone.

Two people were already there. They approached me grinning and excited, saying, "Welcome to NA!" I put out my hand to shake, but before I could escape, I was being hugged. They laughed and said, "We hug here, brother. Hugs, not drugs!" *Man, what kind of cult is this?* I wondered.

I picked a spot in the back row and positioned myself on the small chair. The decor was ratty, and I was sure I saw a few large cockroaches looking for shelter. I wished I could join them. I watched as the room filled with young, attractive, and smartly dressed people my age, hugging, high-fiving, and laughing. As the revelry grew, I felt more and more insecure and out of place; I wanted to slither out of there but knew I had to stay.

Holding nothing back, young men and women shared their stories or current struggles—so much pain, horror, and loss. I could relate to every word. My worst fear became a reality when the person running the meeting asked me to share. I cannot recall exactly what I said, but it was something about not having a problem and then asking her to sponsor me. The room immediately exploded into laughter. I was told, "Keep comin' back. You're in the right place!"

I was mortified and confused, and I did not like being laughed at. At the end of the meeting I got a white chip, which signified I would try the program; I did not have high hopes,

> **But the fruit of the Spirit is love, joy, peace, longsuffering, gentleness, goodness, faith, meekness, temperance: against such there is no law.**
>
> —GALATIANS 5:22 (KJV)

though. Scott, the boyfriend of the female speaker, came over and offered to sponsor me. A sponsor guides a newcomer in the recovery process. He wore a thick gold chain with a large Star of David, indicating his Jewish heritage, same as me. What are the chances of that?

Scott gave me his number and told me it was good twenty-four hours a day, seven days a week, and to call him before I used—meaning drugs or alcohol. His advice to me that night was:

1. Get on your knees in the morning and ask God to keep you sober, then thank Him at night.
2. Don't use under any circumstances; take one day at a time.
3. Make ninety meetings in ninety days.

I told him I didn't believe in God and he explained to me that the program was spiritual—not religious—and that the only stipulation is that I find a loving higher power.

I met with Scott several times that week. I was a full-on mess, carrying skeletons of the past, depression, guilt, and crippling self-pity. One night after a meeting, he told me he loved me as we were hugging goodbye. I was shocked but believed he meant it. He had been clean for five years; I respected and admired him. After that we always ended our meeting with a hug and that affirmation: "Love you, brother."

Over the next six to nine months, I made meetings and tried to practice the first three steps of the program, which basically state that I can't, but He (God) can, and I think I'll let Him. Scott was always there to persuade me not to give up, to help pick me up from deep self-pity. He listened when I was contemplating suicide. Getting clean really sucked! Scott seemed to have the answers, and he saw through all my cons.

I had never met anyone with the wisdom and insight he had. I frequently didn't listen to him and was always argumentative. He would just smile or laugh at me and ask things like, "What did you learn, buddy?" Or he'd say: "You're doing great; you're right where you're supposed to be. If you didn't use today, you're a winner." Even though I did slip up and used drugs maybe ten times, Scott would smile, welcome me back to the program, and tell he loved me.

When he would come and get me after binges, he showed patience, compassion, and unconditional love beyond my comprehension. This love and tolerance were not confined to Scott. Every person at the NA meetings seemed to be filled with love, joy, peace, faith, and kindness. There was something supernatural going on at those meetings, the conferences, and the late-night diner social gatherings. Junkies, thieves, and people who survived every form of evil were now shining with God's presence. It seemed all strife and animus were put aside if one of us was in need.

Still, I could not shake the constant emptiness and loneliness. Shame and guilt would crush me or fear would cripple me. Only drugs or alcohol would provide relief. My last binge ended badly on Easter Sunday, landing me in a rehab center. A few weeks in I was weeping and suicidal. I prayed one last time in desperation. I cursed God and told Him if He existed, I needed Him now.

Something happened right then; I saw, heard, and felt God's presence, a love and peace beyond comprehension. I heard and felt Him say, "You will never drink again, my son." That was spring 1983. I never drank again.

I left the inpatient facility a week after my encounter with God. I told Scott what had happened, and he helped me complete the program's twelve steps. I began to see that everything that happened had a divine origin. God had been there all along, protecting, guiding, and preparing me for redemption. Scott was acting as His hands, His heart, and His voice, expressing true unconditional love and compassion. I was renewed, molded into a new creation by God. I had been born again. I had become a man who was seeking and doing God's will every day.

I dedicated myself to the cause, telling my story in rehabilitation centers, medical detoxes, and prisons. I went on twelve step calls to prospective future members to present a way out. I sponsored several men doing exactly what I learned from Scott. After ten years of sobriety at age twenty-nine, I joined the Navy, got married, and moved to Florida. I raised two children, served my country honorably for twenty-four years, and received a bachelor of arts in mathematics and environmental sciences.

Therefore if any man be in Christ, he is a new creature: old things are passed away; behold, all things are become new.

—2 CORINTHIANS 5:17 (KJV)

It was during these years that I received word from Scott's sponsor that he was found dead in a hotel room with a young woman. They had both overdosed shooting cocaine and heroin. This was the last lesson I learned from Scott—that no one is immune or invincible, that drugs and alcohol kill. We are all only one slip away from tragedy: "But for the grace of God there go I."

Scott was responsible for saving my life and countless others. I would have been dead and gone long ago if God had not

GOD'S GIFT OF SIGHT

— By Tez Brooks —

THERE'S MORE TO sight than what man can view with the human eye. Spiritual sight is much more critical. John 3:3 says that unless one is born again, he cannot see the kingdom of God. That's called spiritual blindness, according to Ephesians 4:17–18, and it leads to eternal separation from God. But if men or women keep their eyes on Jesus, Hebrews 12:1–3 says that people can set aside sins that easily entangle and run the race set before them with endurance. The body's literal eyesight is temporary, lasting only until this life is over—but spiritual vision is eternal.

worked through Scott and others to save me. On this journey I learned a lot about God's character. I've seen numerous miracles and have found significant truth in God's Word. I met Him in Scott, heard Him that night in the rehab center, and now feel Him living within me.

A Note from the Editors

We hope you enjoyed *Signs & Wonders,* published by Guideposts. For over 75 years, Guideposts, a nonprofit organization, has been driven by a vision of a world filled with hope. We aspire to be the voice of a trusted friend, a friend who makes you feel more hopeful and connected.

By making a purchase from Guideposts, you join our community in touching millions of lives, inspiring them to believe that all things are possible through faith, hope, and prayer. Your continued support allows us to provide uplifting resources to those in need. Whether through our communities, websites, apps, or publications, we inspire our audiences, bring them together, and comfort, uplift, entertain, and guide them.

Visit us at guideposts.org to learn more.

We would love to hear from you. Write us at Guideposts, P.O. Box 5815, Harlan, Iowa 51593 or call us at (800) 932-2145. Did you love *Signs & Wonders?* Leave a review for this product on guideposts.org/shop. Your feedback helps others in our community find relevant products.

Find inspiration, find faith, find Guideposts.

Shop our best sellers and favorites at

guideposts.org/shop